TERESA OF JESUS
WOMAN · PROPHET · MYSTIC

*A Woman's Transformation through
Her Relationship with Christ*

María Rosaura González Casas, S.T.J.

TRANSLATED BY
JUDY ROXBOROUGH, S.T.J.

ICS Publications
Institute of Carmelite Studies
Washington, D.C.

ICS Publications
2131 Lincoln Road NE
Washington, DC 20002-1199
www.icspublications.org

© Washington Province of Discalced Carmelites, Inc., 2020
Published with Ecclesiastical Approval

This book was originally published in Spanish in 2007 by Editorial Claretiana, Argentina. © Editorial Claretiana, 2007, ISBN: 978-950-512-637-8.

Cover and text design and pagination by Rose Design
Printed in the United States of America

Cover photo from main chapel window of Generalate,
Society of St. Teresa of Jesus, Rome

Library of Congress Cataloging-in-Publication Data

Names: Gonzalez Casas, Maria Rosaura, author. | Roxborough, Judy, translator.
Title: Teresa of Jesus : woman, prophet, mystic : a woman's transformation through her relationship with Christ / Maria Rosaura Gonzalez Casas, S.T.J. ; translated by Judy Roxborough, S.T.J..
Other titles: Fuerza de la mujer en Teresa de Jesús. English
Identifiers: LCCN 2020016852 (print) | LCCN 2020016853 (ebook) | ISBN 9781939272508 (trade paperback) | ISBN 9781939272478 (ebook)
Subjects: LCSH: Teresa, of Avila, Saint, 1515-1582.
Classification: LCC BX4700.T4 G6613 2020 (print) | LCC BX4700.T4 (ebook) | DDC 271/.97102--dc23
LC record available at https://lccn.loc.gov/2020016852
LC ebook record available at https://lccn.loc.gov/2020016853

pbk: 978-1-939272-50-8
ebook: 978-1-939272-47-8

5 4 3 2 1

Contents

Translations
and Abbreviations

Scripture quotations are from the *New Revised Standard Version Bible: Catholic Edition, Anglicized Text*, copyright ©1999, 1995, 1989, Division of Christian Education of the National Council of Churches of Christ of the United States of America. Used with permission. All rights reserved.

St. Teresa of Ávila

All quotations from the works of Teresa of Ávila are taken from *The Collected Works of St. Teresa of Ávila*, trans. Kieran Kavanaugh, O.C.D., and Otilio Rodriguez, O.C.D., 3 vols. (Washington, D.C.: ICS Publications, 1976–1985, 1987, 2012).

The following abbreviations will be used in references to Teresa's works:

  S *Soliloquies*
  F *The Book of the Foundations*
 IC *The Interior Castle*
  L *The Book of Her Life*
Ltr *Letters*
ST *The Spiritual Testimonies*
 W *The Way of Perfection*

In general, when cited in abbreviated form, the abbreviation of the work is given. The first number refers to the chapter, and the second number refers to the paragraph. Thus, W 3.5 refers to *The Way of Perfection*, chapter 3, paragraph 5. Regarding *The Interior Castle*, the first number refers to the dwelling place, the second number refers to the chapter, and the third number refers to the paragraph. Thus, IC 3.4.2 refers to the third dwelling place, chapter 4, paragraph 2.

Vatican Documents

All quotations from the documents of the Second Vatican Council are taken from Austin Flannery, ed., *The Basic Sixteen Documents of Vatican II* (Northport, NY: Costello Publishing, 1996).

The following abbreviations will be used in references to the documents of Vatican II:

DV   *Dei Verbum* (Dogmatic Constitution on Divine Revelation)

GS   *Gaudium et Spes* (Pastoral Constitution on the Church in the Modern World)

Foreword

n this new work María Rosaura González Casas offers the hope we Christians need to confront the cultural, institutional, and structural barriers that limit our capacity to attain the freedom we are called to exercise as creatures made in the image of God.

We are immersed in a world of fear, terrorism, hunger, poverty, and religious hatred in the midst of those driven by unspeakable greed for power and wealth. We come from two world wars, the Holocaust, the atomic bombs in Hiroshima and Nagasaki, the increasing threat of widespread world hunger, the expanding refugee crisis, and other present-day tragedies and horrors. Our civilization is changing under the influence of postmodernism. Values appear to have lost the meaning they had long held while the religious metanarratives are severely challenged by indifference and disbelief. How can I say that a book about Teresa of Jesus could carry any weight to give us hope to face our world?

Teresa's days do not seem much better to me. Europeans had "discovered" and begun exploring the Americas twenty-three years before she was born. Europe became immersed in fantasies of incredible exuberance and wealth and started the frantic conquest of the "New World." In 1492, the same year as Columbus' American landing, the forces of Ferdinand and Isabella defeated the Moors in Granada. That very year they decided to expel all Jews from their territories, for religious motives. The Jews had to either convert to Catholicism or leave in four months. It was suggested that the Jewish presence would interfere with the transformation of Marranos, or conversos, converted Jews, into good Christians.

Fear of heretics gripped Spain. In 1481, Ferdinand and Isabella established the Spanish Inquisition to investigate the purity of the faith of Jewish and Muslim converts to Catholicism. These groups, known as conversos if Jewish, Moriscos if Muslims, were suspected of having feigned a conversion of convenience while continuing to practice their previous beliefs. Soon inquisitors began to suspect that almost anybody capable of thinking or writing must be guilty of one type of heresy or another. Ironically, women could not be suspected of heretical theories because they were not allowed to study. Yet the *Malleus Maleficarum* (The hammer of witches), printed in 1486, focused on the sexual proclivity of women to obtain satisfaction from the devil himself. They were interrogated, sexually tortured, and finally killed, and their families as well—as a way of saving their souls! Then came Martin Luther, with his ninety-five theses posted on the Wittenberg castle church on October 31, 1517, when Teresa was just two years old. The Reformation continued to spread, and the Inquisition renewed its efforts to contain the heresy.

The events listed above are enough to convince me—and I hope the reader—that the Spain in which Teresa was born was a religious police state in the hands of the Inquisition in connivance with the king and the court. Religious fear infiltrated the air people breathed. Any wrong move or any suspicious sentence could land a person in the hands of an inquisitor. Teresa herself, in her efforts to avoid the inquisitors, wrote under vigilant supervision. Yet she was denounced to the Inquisition seven times.

In those dark historical circumstances, being a woman was less than being a second-class citizen. Women were servants of their husbands, economically enslaved by the law, and prohibited from any aspiration to be educated and to exercise their intelligence. Those who found refuge in convents experienced many as places to lock up women for life, against their will, under the power of the male benefactors of the monastery. To put it briefly, women had no freedom to be themselves. Submission to men—whether father, brother, or husband—was their destiny.

In the midst of this dismal situation for women, Teresa of Jesus performed a remarkable miracle: she became fully herself, free from the shackles her culture, her church, and the Inquisition were ready to place on her. In chapter 2 of this text, María Rosaura González Casas describes Teresa's struggle: "Teresa was longing for a freedom that had been taken from her (see L 27.13). The contrast between the need to cry out the abundance of God and the feeling of being 'bound with so many chains' (IC 4.6.3) that kept her from doing so was a constant drama, a tension that breaks out repeatedly in her writings." Teresa liberated herself from such chains by being faithful to her nature as a woman committed to relating to God and to others. Her theologically unimpeachable relational manner of loving God and others freed her from the convolutions of theological doctrines and, to a point, from the Inquisition. She based her undeniable dignity as a woman on the biblical text, asserting that we all, men and women, are created in the image of God. Women too are made in the image of God.

Her life itinerary as a person and as a mystic is based on her effort to know herself realistically in her way of relating to God, whose image is at the center of her being. Such knowledge is strictly experiential and is the source of Teresa's claim that she knows well what she is talking about. Her religious relational experiences with her God and the humanity of Christ lead her to invest her entire being as a woman in the relational and mutual love with God. From chapter 6 in this text, we see that love is the key: "The images that Teresa presents reveal all her feminine being: as a spouse in love with and completely surrendered to the other, with nothing reserved for herself; and as a sister and fruitful mother concerned with the salvation of souls. She becomes an icon of the feminine face of the church, those women and men in love with the Beloved and capable of surrendering themselves totally to God, fruitful in their apostolic mission."

Teresa liberated herself from her cultural chains by allowing her feminine being to remain faithful to her God and to her neighbor as a loving woman. Teresa invites all Christians to be "enamored," that is, to be involved in a loving relationship with God and all others. Through her love she liberated herself and invites all of us to free ourselves from cultural constraints standing in our way of fulfilling the two basic commandments: to love God and to love neighbor. The conclusion is clear: Teresa was able to create "a new paradigm of women in the church" (see introduction), one that keeps crying out until this day.

María Rosaura González Casas deserves our gratitude for looking at Teresa as a woman who became a great saint and theologian because she held tightly to her identity as a female person made in the image of God. We must also thank her for giving us in this book a detailed and well-structured itinerary of Teresa's journey as a woman searching to love her God.

ANA-MARIA RIZZUTO, M.D.
Training and Supervising Analyst Emerita,
Psychoanalytic Institute of New England
Needham, Massachusetts

Introduction

Teresa de Ahumada y Cepeda—later known, by her choice, as Teresa of Jesus and now as St. Teresa of Ávila—was, above all, a woman who searched for an encounter with God, and her search was not in vain. Once she encountered God, she wanted nothing more than to put him at the center of her life and proclaim his greatness. Driven by this burning desire and guided by the Spirit, she came to live a profound union with God and with the people she related to. In her writings and in her labor to reform the Carmelite Order, we can discover aspects of her spiritual experience and her radical evangelical determination.

As writer and founder, Teresa suffered the consequences of offering with her life a new paradigm of women in the church. Like Jesus and many others who followed the call of God, she was criticized, rejected, reprimanded, and even brought before the Inquisition seven times. Yet the truth of her experience was eventually proved through the fire of opposition. Her writings, translated into more than two hundred languages, have become spiritual classics that continue to inspire all those who seek the living God.

In the twentieth century alone, there have been more than 5,000 studies published on St. Teresa. In the abundant bibliography that exists, however, there are few investigations that treat her life and works from the historical-sociocultural perspective of women, or that analyze the characteristics of her feminine nature as shown in her life process. The theme of Teresa as woman has been treated primarily from other perspectives. In nineteenth-century Spain, Teresa was promoted with much enthusiasm, especially by St. Henry de Ossó, a great Teresian apostle who propagated her works and doctrine, valuing her as woman and spiritual mother.[1] But the first study on the theme of Teresa as woman did not fully capture the strategies of the Teresian lexicon; rather, it considered the feminine characteristics from a passive perspective.[2] In later years, investigations appeared that began to suggest that rereading her works through the lens of woman could cast new light on the understanding of her work and mission.[3] There were investigations of her literary style, which was understandably influenced by her being a woman of the sixteenth century; her astute strategies as a writer;[4] her

---

1. St. Henry de Ossó, prolific writer and catechist, founded the Society of St. Teresa of Jesus, to continue her spirituality and message, especially through education. Today the society, known in the United States as the Teresian Sisters, exists in more than twenty countries throughout the world.

2. Dominique Deneuville, *Sainte Thérèse d'Ávila et la femme* (Paris: Editions du Chalet, 1963).

3. Teófanes Egido, "Santa Teresa y su condición de mujer," *Surge* 40 (1982): 155–275; Ulrich Dobhan, "Teresa de Jesús y la emancipación de la mujer," in *Actas del Congreso Internacional Teresiano*, ed. Teófanes Egido, 121–36, vol. 1 (Salamanca, Spain: Universidad de Salamanca, 1983); Salvador Ros García, "Santa Teresa en su condición histórica de mujer espiritual," in *Perfil histórico de Santa Teresa*, ed. Teófanes Egido, 147–48. (Madrid: Editorial de Espiritualidad, 1981).

4. Rosa Rossi, *Teresa d'Ávila. Biografía di una scrittrice* (Rome: Editori Riuniti, 1983); Alison Weber, *Teresa of Ávila and the Rhetoric of Femininity* (Princeton, N.J.: Princeton University Press, 1990); Carole Slade, *St. Teresa of Ávila: Author of a Heroic Life* (Berkeley: University of California Press, 1995).

characteristics as a woman educator;[5] and her difficult situation as a woman in the church.[6]

Reading Teresa with new perspectives makes more evident the contributions that she can give to the historic moment in which we live. For example, if we focus from a horizontal perspective, we find her anthropological and psychological vision, with all the dynamism that hinders or favors the way of transformation in Christ. If we focus from a vertical perspective, we can deduce Teresa's own approach to theology and spirituality.

I propose, then, new perspectives in the analysis of her writings, in particular of *The Interior Castle*. Teresa's objective in writing her highest work was to teach her nuns the way of prayer by means of her own "systematized" experience. We find ourselves with a book of spiritual theology, with Teresa as a skillful teacher on this road. She knows how to spot inner resistances and movements in order to listen to and follow God's call. At the same time, she considers the inner dynamics that generate the process of relationship with God, making her work a sixteenth-century treatment of psychology.

This book will look at relationships as a point of encounter and dialogue between Teresian spiritual theology and psychology. I have divided it into two parts. In the first, "Teresa of Jesus: Woman in Her Sociohistorical Context," I give an overview of society in the sixteenth century in order to help

---

5. Jesús Barrena, *Teresa de Jesús. Una Mujer Educadora* (Ávila, Spain: Institución Gran Duque de Alba de la Diputación Provincial, 2000).

6. Tomás Álvarez, "Santa Teresa y las mujeres en la Iglesia: Glosa al texto teresiano de Camino 3," *Monte Carmelo* 89 (1981): 121–32; Gillian Ahlgren, *Teresa of Ávila and the Politics of Sanctity* (New York: Cornell University Press, 1996).

us understand and imagine how Teresa would be viewed as a woman of that age and what currents of thought may have influenced her. We will enter into the concept of woman in the culture of her time to see how she had to confront this ideology until she could unmask it down to its very roots. In her feminine humanity, Teresa supports particular characteristics that I have tried to note, such as her relational aspect.[7] We will see how the aspect of connection and empathy forms part of Teresa's style of communication. This first part will provide the necessary background to permit the reader to enter with greater understanding into the second part, "*The Interior Castle.*"

The Interior Castle is a doctrinal book that was formed in the womb of the experiences Teresa lived and wrote about in *The Book of Her Life.* In it she presents countless themes as worthy aspects of study. Here, however, I have taken the relational aspect from the feminine perspective as the analytical key. It is through the relationship that her process of human and divine maturation develops in the seven dwelling places of the castle, making a true synthesis of unity between the love of God and the love of her sisters and brothers. We will be able to see "the divinization of the human" and the "humanization of the divine" that the Teresian path implies. We have the advantage

---

7. In various studies of psychoanalytic character and biogenetics, it is argued that one of the characteristics that mark the difference between the feminine and masculine gender is that empathy and connection are an element of clear feminine identity. See Nancy Chodorow, "Gender, Relation and Difference in Psychoanalytic Perspective," in *Feminism and Psychoanalytic Theory,* 99–113 (New Haven, Conn.: Yale University Press, 1989); and Simon Baron-Cohen, *The Essential Difference: Men and Women and the Extreme Male Brain* (London: Penguin, 2003). This does not mean that no men are empathetic or that all women are, but that empathy is a characteristic that prevails in the population of women at large.

that the narrator is a woman, so that in her writings we can see her own personal deveopment and unravel what she thinks about herself, what she aspires to, how she lives her experiences.[8]

The method we will follow is fundamentally an analytical reading of Teresa's writings, in particular, the book *The Interior Castle*. For a better clarification of the text, we will seek points of contact with the experiences narrated in *The Book of Her Life* that are located in the corresponding mansion; we will also use other writings in order to comprehend certain concepts and what Teresa lived and systematized in *The Interior Castle* with the greatest precision possible. The relationship of the soul to God enables her to know herself and also makes possible the transformation of relationships with others as fruit of this encounter.

Drawing close to Teresa's life, to her process and profound experience in this stage of our history, is to drink from a fount that always yields fresh water. Teresa's experience reminds me of Karl Rahner's famous statement that "the Christian of the future will either be a mystic, one who has experienced 'something,' or he will cease to be anything at all."[9] In the light of Teresa's experience, I dare to say that the mystics of today are very human or they are not mystics. I hope that the reader will discover that in these pages.

---

8. Currently the analysis of a person's history and narration is considered a precise instrument, adequate for understanding one's personality, values, and conflicts. A narration can be considered a psychosocial construct. See Cáit O'Dwyer, *Imagining One's Future: A Projective Approach to Christian Maturity* (Rome: Editrice Pontificia Università Gregoriana, 2000).

9. Karl Rahner, "Christian Living Formerly and Today," in Theological Investigations VII, trans. David Bourke (New York: Herder and Herder, 1971), 15 as quoted in Harvey D. Egan, Soundings in the Christian Mystical Tradition (Collegeville, MN: Liturgical Press, 2010), 338.

PART 1

Teresa of Jesus:
WOMAN IN HER
SOCIOHISTORICAL CONTEXT

1

Woman in
Sixteenth-Century Spain

The historical age in which Teresa of Jesus lived marked her deeply, in her way of living as much as in her quest to be united with God and to do God's will. We will look first at the society in which she developed, in order to be able to unravel that era's concept of gender.

Time of Renewal

Teresa's century was a time of change, of fresh air, and also a time that witnessed the birth of opposing currents of thought. When Christopher Columbus opened his heart to America, the "Old World" was also being invaded by new ideas that challenged its ways of thinking. At the same time, a new movement was born, filled with a profound desire for renewal at all levels, earning for this age the name "Renaissance." The Renaissance arrived later in Spain than in the rest of Europe and is placed during the fifteenth and sixteenth centuries, Spain's "Golden Age."[1]

---

1. See Roger Aubenas and Robert Ricard, "El Renacimiento," in *Historia de la Iglesia*, ed. Augustin Fliche and Victor Martin, vol. 17 (Valencia, Spain: EDICEP, 1974), 293–475.

Renewal was promoted in the Spanish church primarily by Cardinal Jimenez de Cisneros, a Franciscan friar who presided over religious life throughout the realm.[2] He supported theological reflection and spiritual experimentation, so that learning was integrated with piety and sacred studies. Thanks to the invention of movable type, Cisneros disseminated religious and spiritual literature. Among the books published in that era were the four-volume *Life of Christ* by the 14th-century Carthusian Ludolph of Saxony (which Teresa read and treasured); in the vernacular, *The Spiritual Ladder* by John Climacus; the *Commentary on the Miserere* by Girolamo Savonarola; the writings of St. Angela of Foligno; *The Book of Special Grace* by St. Gertrude; the *Letters and Prayers* of St. Catherine of Siena; and the Rule of St. Clare. In Toledo in 1512, *Epistolas y Evangelios*, a Spanish translation of the Epistles and Gospels with commentary, was published, as well as the translation of *The Imitation of Christ*. By means of the University of Alcalá, Cisneros promoted culture with a Renaissance spirit and a humanist character, cultivating the study of ancient Middle Eastern languages. Specialists concentrating in biblical philology, both Christians and Jews, collaborated in the edition of the celebrated polyglot Bible in Hebrew, Chaldaic, Greek, and Latin. Alcalá maintained direct contact with European centers and welcomed the trends promoted by Erasmus of Rotterdam, the well-known Catholic humanist, who worked toward reforming the church from within.[3]

---

2. Jimenez de Cisneros, the confessor of Queen Isabella in 1492, became the archbishop of Toledo in 1495, and was named cardinal and inquisitor general in 1507; he died in 1517. See Aubenas and Ricard, "El Renacimiento," 332–37.

3. José M. Javierre, *Juan de la Cruz, un Caso Límite* (Salamanca, Spain: Sigueme, 1991), 355–57.

An age like this, fed by spiritual books and new ways of thinking, gave birth to a sixteenth-century movement in Spain that reached its peak in the Spanish mystics. Its more famous representatives are Teresa of Jesus, John of the Cross, Ignatius of Loyola, and John of Ávila. Yet it also gave birth to a popular movement that transcended the barriers of gender, although briefly, and reproduced some characteristics of the primitive church.[4]

Promotion of Women: Early Steps Meet Frustration

The mood of the age, greatly influenced by Erasmus, fit smoothly with the tendency of the Franciscan cardinal to promote women. Cisneros, the queen's confessor, believed in women and admired their mystical graces and their profound spiritual life.[5] Because of his efforts, women recovered a certain authority as spiritual teachers within the church, and he was therefore designated as "the enthusiastic promoter of feminine piety." In 1516 Erasmus published the *Paraclesis* or *Exhortation to Diligent Study of Scripture*, in which he exhorts all Christians, including women, to study Scripture and the philosophy of Christ.[6] As more complete editions of the Bible were published in

4. See Alison Weber, *Teresa of Ávila and the Rhetoric of Femininity* (Princeton, N.J.: Princeton University Press, 1990), 23.

5. See Aubenas and Ricard, "El Renacimiento," 528–39.

6. Emma de Moreau, Pierre Jourdá, and Pierre Janelle, "La Crisis religiosa del siglo XVI," in *Historia de la Iglesia*, ed. Augustin Fliche and Victor Martin, vol. 18 (Valencia, Spain: EDICEP, 1978), 125–26.

the vernacular, women gained access to the word of God.[7] The desire to live interior prayer came to life in a popular movement: "The girls with water jugs under their arms were bringing their [prayer] manuals; the fruit and vegetable sellers were reading them while they were weighing and selling their goods."[8] Groups of men and women were formed, lay and religious, who met in their homes to comment on the Scripture. Although they didn't have a unified doctrine, they shared the belief that the Holy Spirit would "illuminate" them in understanding Sacred Scripture. These ideas later gave birth to what in Spain would be called *Alumbradismo*.[9]

---

7. Teresa did not have the Spanish translation of the whole Bible at hand, but she was able to have some books and, in particular, commentaries. We know this because after the debate of the theme in the Council of Trent in the fourth session, 1546, Spanish theologians pronounced it would be best that they not make complete translations of the Bible. The people normally had access to Spanish editions of some books of the Bible and commentaries. See Tomás Álvarez, ed., *Diccionario de Santa Teresa* (Burgos, Spain: Monte Carmelo, 2002), 83; and *Gran Enciclopedia Universal* (Madrid: Espasa Calpe, 2004), 1584.

8. Daniel de Pablo Maroto, *Dinámica de la Oración* (Madrid: Editorial de Espiritualidad, 1973), 89.

9. Enrique Llamas, O.C.D., has investigated the Inquisition of the sixteenth century. See Enrique Llamas, "Santa Teresa de Jesús ante la Inquisición Española," *Ephemerides Carmeliticae* 13 (1962): 518–65. In his book *Santa Teresa de Jesús y la Inquisición Española* (Madrid: Consejo Superior de Investigaciones Cientificas, Instituto "Francisco Suarez," 1972), he concludes that the true Alumbradism was not a phenomenon so universal as the Inquisition accusers had painted, and he asks for a new study that would reverse the process: to judge the attitude and truth of the judges. See Enrique Llamas, "Teresa de Jesús y los alumbrados. Hacia una revisión del 'alumbradismo' español del siglo XVI," in *Actas del Congreso Internacional Teresiano*, ed. Teófanes Egido, 137–67, vol. 1 (Salamanca, Spain: Universidad de Salamanca, 1983).

In these prayer groups, some women took leading roles,[10] but since they did not have instruction (because it was not permitted for women), they had no way to describe their spiritual experiences in the terminology of the learned. Often their expression appeared to be outside the established orthodoxy, and they were therefore suspected of *Alumbradismo.*

The convergence of several events and movements in 1517 brought about a profound change in the direction of church history: Cardinal Cisneros died; Martin Luther's rebellion began in Germany with the publication of his theses in Wittenberg; followers of Erasmus were suspected of being anticlerical; and the persecution of the Jewish converts intensified.[11] In 1525 the first edict condemning the Alumbrados was published.

The Spirituals, the Learned, and the Alumbrados: The Inquisition as Background

In this situation we can identify three different movements. One was promoted by Cisneros and his followers, emphasizing

---

10. Among these were Isabel of the Cross, Maria de Cazalla, who preached the word to women in her house in Guadalajara; Francisca Hernandez, who exercised great influence on the preachers of Valladolid; and the Beata Catalina de Cardona, who knew St. Teresa.

11. The decree ordering the expulsion of the Jews had been given on March 31, 1492, having as principal reason the protection of the Catholic faith. Between 100,000 and 200,000 left. Later the statutes of purity of blood appeared, which meant not having Jewish or Muslim ancestors. See Albert Sicroff, *Los estatutos de limpieza de sangre. Controversias entre los siglos XV–XVII* (Madrid: Taurus, 1985).

the experience of the evangelical life and relationship with God. Women also belonged to this movement, and Cisneros calls them "*los espirituales*" (the spiritual ones). Teresa of Jesus, Ignatius of Loyola, John of Ávila, John of the Cross, and many others were in this group. While emphasizing aspects of experience and of an integrated life, they did not reject the criteria of objectivity that the church provided; on the contrary, they insisted that faith had to be lived, it had to become experience.

Another movement, in clear opposition to the first, was that of the learned, or the official theologians, for whom prayer raised the suspicion of illuminist (*Alumbradismo*) phenomena and of the seeds of Lutheranism. This confrontation between the learned and the spirituals was truly a war. When confronted with the longing to be with God in a personal way, the theologians resisted, using the powerful weapon of the Inquisition against the spirituals, who found themselves defenseless and on the verge of being considered heretics.[12] This explains something of the hostilities toward some of the outstanding reformers of the age: the gentle and learned Dominican theologian, Archbishop Bartoloméo Carranza; John of Ávila, parish priest and apostle, who worked to reform the priesthood; Francis Borgia, Jesuit leader and one of Teresa's confessors; and Teresa of Jesus herself.

The third movement was the popular one, in which people without formal education earnestly sought God. Many of the women known as *beatas* were in this group.

The convergence of these historic events, together with the Inquisition as a means of control, unleashed a persecution of the

---

12. See Ulrich Dobhan, "Teresa de Jesús y la emancipación de la mujer," in *Actas del Congreso Internacional Teresiano*, ed. Teófanes Egido, 121–36, vol. 1 (Salamanca, Spain: Universidad de Salamanca, 1983), 123.

spirituals,[13] who were suspected of being associated with Luther's Protestant movement because they read the Bible and some other books in the vernacular. Because the spirituals were seen as possibly heretical, they were regarded as a threat to the unity of the Spanish church. If a woman was instructed in the Bible, she was suspected of being an *Alumbrada* or a Lutheran. Jewish converts also suffered in this persecution, because it was thought they might return to Judaism after their confession of faith.

Another Dominican, Melchior Cano, generally regarded as the greatest theologian of his time, was one of the most outstanding figures of the age. In 1559 he condemned the catechism of his fellow Dominican, Bishop Carranza:

> Experience tells us that to give a reading [of Sacred Scripture] all or in part in the vernacular has done damage to women and to the foolish. So have the heretics done. For wanting to make the Germans into scholars, opening their eyes to see what their ancestors had never seen, they began to avail themselves and fashion the errors that they later sowed. The tree of that theological science, however beautiful it seems to the eyes and to the taste, however much the serpent promotes that the eyes of the people be opened with this tidbit, and however much women lay claim with insatiable appetite to eat this fruit [of Sacred Scripture], it is necessary to prohibit it and seal it with fire so that people [do] not come in contact with it.[14]

---

13. They were persecuted particularly during the Council of Trent, when the threat of the Protestants in the north of Europe was stronger.

14. Fermin Caballero, *Vida del Ilustrísimo Melchor Cano. Conquenses ilustres*, vol. 2, 536–39, cited in Daniel de Pablo Maroto, "Santa Teresa y el Protestantismo Español," in *Perfil histórico de Santa Teresa*, ed. Teófanes Egido (Madrid: Editorial de Espiritualidad, 1981), 147–48.

Thus it was taught that if a woman wanted to pray, she should use only vocal prayer; she was not capable of more and was in danger of deluding herself. Father Domingo Bañez, censor of the book of Teresa's life, wrote, "There is only one thing in this book to pay attention to, and with reason enough to examine it very well, which is that it has many revelations and visions, which are always to be greatly feared, especially in women, who are quick to believe that they are from God and call them holy."[15]

What Concept of Woman?

We can see the idea of woman in the sixteenth century in the book *The Perfect Wife* by Luis de León, an Augustinian friar who was the first to publish the *Works of Teresa of Jesus*:

It is fitting that women be esteemed in being silent, those for whom it is convenient to conceal their lack of knowledge, as well as those who can reveal what they know; because in all it is not only a pleasing condition, but an obligatory virtue, being silent and speaking little; for just as nature made women so that they be closed up, keeping house, so are they obliged to close their mouths; because speaking is born of understanding, and words are nothing but images or signs of what the spirit conceives in itself; for whereas, just as Nature did not make the good and honest woman for the study of science, nor for managing difficult matters, but for only one simple and domestic office,

---

15. Domingo Bañez, "Censura en el autógrafo de la Vida de Sta. Teresa," in *Obras Completas de Santa Teresa*, ed. Efrén de la Madre De Dios and Otger Steggink (Madrid: Editorial Católica, 1977), 190.

so it limited her understanding and consequently fixed her words and reasoning ability.[16]

Thus, in the religious culture of this time a woman was considered "virtuous" if she concealed her knowledge and kept quiet. It was thought that woman "by nature" had not been equipped to reason or understand, much less to study the sciences. A little later, de León continues:

> And as God did not even give them the ingenuity that most businesses require, nor the strength necessary for war or working in the field, they are to measure themselves according to what they are, being content with what is their lot, familiar with the home and going about the house, *for God made them only for that*. At birth the Chinese twist girls' feet, binding them so that when they become women they won't have straight limbs to go outside; those twisted limbs are sufficient for walking around the house. As men are for the public, so women are for enclosure; and as it is for men to speak and to go outside, so for women it is to be locked up and covered up.[17]

The sanctity of woman consisted in submitting herself to her spouse, occupying herself with spinning and staying home. She was supposed to be content with this situation because it was held that God made women to live this way. Francisco de Osuna, from whom Teresa learned her first steps in prayer from his book *The Third Spiritual Alphabet*, wrote in 1531, "Whenever you see your woman walking many stations [of

---

16. Luis de León and Félix García, *La Casada Perfecta* (Mexico City, Mexico: Aguilar, 1976), 320.

17. León and García, 324 (emphasis added).

the cross], giving herself to devotions and putting on saintly airs, close the door. And if that is not enough, if she is young, break her leg; for a cripple could go to heaven from her house without going about looking for dubious holiness. It is enough that a woman hear a sermon and if she wants to do more, let her read a book while she spins, and seat herself at the hand of her husband."[18]

In summary, the historical ecclesial context in which Teresa developed was contradictory. Desires to promote women were interwoven with an environment that was fundamentally misogynistic, born of a preconception of what it means to be female. It was believed that women's rationality was inferior (even though they were not permitted to study, whereby they might demonstrate the contrary!), that they were easily deceived in prayer, and that they had difficulties with discernment and moral judgment. On account of all that, if a woman read the Bible or had some experience of prayer, she was suspected of Alumbradism and Lutheranism. Women were regarded as more vulnerable to temptations of the devil in the flesh,[19] and the ideal of sanctity for a woman was to be silent, to submit to her husband, and to stay home and dedicate herself to spinning. Teresa speaks to us of this submission, contrasting it with how the Lord regards women:

---

18. Cited in Ros García, "Santa Teresa," 67.

19. "In them reason is not so strong as it is in men, who with the reason that is greater in them, restrain the passions of the flesh; but women are more flesh than spirit, and therefore are more inclined to that than to the spirit." Martin de Córdoba, *Tratado que se intitula Jardín de las nobles doncellas*, ed. Fernando Rubio (Madrid: Atlas, 1946), 91. Written at the end of the sixteenth century and cited in Gillian Ahlgren, *Teresa of Ávila and the Politics of Sanctity* (New York: Cornell University Press, 1996), 7.

"They say that for a woman to be a good wife toward her husband she must be sad when he is sad, and joyful when he is joyful, even though she may not be so. (See what subjection you have been freed from, sisters!) The Lord, without deception, truly acts in such a way with us. He is the one who submits, and He wants you to be the lady with authority to rule; He submits to your will" (W 26.4).[20]

---

20. Also, "the great favor God has granted them in choosing them for Himself and freeing them from being subject to a man, who is often the death of them and who could also be, God forbid, the death of their souls" (F 31.46).

2

Teresa of Jesus (1515–1582)

Teresa has been held more as an object of admiration than as someone close to us, a real person who can be encountered, and a mediator in the journey of following Christ. Her remarkable popularity and beguiling personality, together with the desire to exalt her, have introduced in her story certain "false extrahistorical" elements: proclaiming her "santa de la raza" (roughly, "the best of our culture and of our country" –Trans.) or affirming that she was proud of her noble heritage.[1] In reality, the latest investigations confirm that Teresa did not exactly belong to the Spanish *hidalgos* (the nobility), nor did she have the desired "purity of blood"; rather, her roots are a mixture of races, cultures, and religions,

---

1. See Teófanes Egido, "El tratamiento historográfico de Santa Teresa. Inercias y revisiones," in *Perfil histórico de Santa Teresa*, ed. Teófanes Egido, 13–31 (Madrid: Editorial de Espiritualidad, 1981), as well as José Garcia Oro, "Reformas y observancias: crisis y renovación de la vida religiosa española durante el Renacimiento," in *Perfil histórico de Santa Teresa*, ed. Teófanes Egido, 32–55 (Madrid: Editorial de Espiritualidad, 1981); Andrés Melquíades, "Erasmismo y Tradición," in *Perfil histórico de Santa Teresa*, ed. Teófanes Egido, 95–117 (Madrid: Editorial de Espiritualidad, 1981); Daniel

making her more ordinary, closer to our own world, with its many cultures and religions.

The vast bibliography dedicated to her testifies to the persistence of the historical inaccuracy that has long separated us from the concrete, human Teresa. Beginning with the celebration of the fourth centenary of her death in 1982, the search for the real Teresa deepened, and new approaches appeared. In recent years some have begun to reread her message through new lenses, drawing closer to her person and doctrine.[2]

A New Reading of Her Life

The discovery that Teresa's grandfather, some uncles, and even her father, Don Alonso Sánchez de Cepeda, were Jewish

---

de Pablo Maroto, "Santa Teresa y el Protestantismo Español," in *Perfil histórico de Santa Teresa*, ed. Teófanes Egido, 119–51 (Madrid: Editorial de Espiritualidad, 1981); and Enrique Llamas, "Teresa de Jesús y la religiosidad popular," in *Perfil histórico de Santa Teresa*, ed. Teófanes Egido, 57–94 (Madrid: Editorial de Espiritualidad, 1981). See also all the work of updating by Maximiliano Herráiz, ed., *Obras completas de Santa Teresa de Jesús* (Salamanca, Spain: Ediciones Sigueme, 1997); and the extensive studies of investigation, recovery, and interpretation accomplished fundamentally by Tomás Álvarez.

2. John Welch, *Spiritual Pilgrims: Carl Jung and Teresa of Ávila* (New York: Paulist Press, 1982); Alison Weber, *Teresa of Ávila and the Rhetoric of Femininity* (Princeton, N.J.: Princeton University Press, 1990); Mary Frohlich, *The Intersubjectivity of the Mystic* (Atlanta: Scholars Press, 1993); Carole Slade, *St. Teresa of Ávila: Author of a Heroic Life* (Berkeley: University of California Press, 1995); Gillian Ahlgren, *Teresa of Ávila and the Politics of Sanctity* (New York: Cornell University Press, 1996); Michel de Goedt, *Il Cristo di Teresa* (Vatican City: Libreria editrice vaticana, 1997); Ciro Garcia, *Santa Teresa de Jesús: Nuevas claves de Lectura* (Burgos, Spain: Monte Carmelo, 1998); Juan Antonio Marcos, *Mística y Subversiva. Teresa de Jesús* (Madrid: Editorial de Espiritualidad, 2001); Edward Howells, *John of the Cross and Teresa of Ávila, Spain: Mystical Knowing and Self-hood* (New York: Crossroad, 2002); Julienne McLean, *Towards Mystical Union* (London: St. Paul's, 2003); Antonio Mas Arrondo, *Acercar el cielo* (Cantabria, Spain: Sal Terrae, 2004).

converts, expands the horizon for rereading her work.[3] We can understand her struggles and suffering with concerns about "honor" and the life of appearances.[4] She knew the efforts that her father had made to cover the humiliations and marks that her grandfather, "the Toledan," had suffered doing public penance (wearing a sanbenito, a long, yellow tunic, as a sign of penance in processions of reconciliation) through the streets of Toledo, the most aristocratic city in Spain.[5] Surely Teresa knew that they had moved from another city and that her grandfather had tried to conceal his roots by leaving behind the business of commerce and renting property, work associated with Jews. In addition, the Cepedas bought their title of nobility and whatever was necessary to live as one of the best families in Ávila.

These recent discoveries in turn changed the preconceptions formed about Teresa's family. Once regarded as "an old noble Christian family with pure blood," in reality they belonged to the cruelly marginalized group of Jewish converts.

---

3. Jews reconciled in 1485, the year of grace in Toledo, with the consequent public penances and humiliations in the parish of Santa Leocadia. See Egido, "El tratamiento," 24. Furthermore, Teresa's grandfather, Don Juan Sánchez de Toledo, recanted and "Judaized" (returned to Jewish practice). Considered the ultimate sin of that time, it was punishable by being burned at the stake. Only through confessing could there be penitence and pardon.

4. The phrase "black honor," *negra honra* in Spanish, referred to a false sense of honor that sought to maintain an outward appearance of nobility; it had nothing to do with being honorable. –Trans.

5. The sanbenito, a long tunic, generally yellow with a red cross in the center, exposed the procession of penitents to the sneers of the crowd, and even though it could mean terrible humiliation for the rich merchant, it freed him from whipping, life in prison, or auto-da-fé, the final test: being burned at the stake. See José M. Javierre, *Teresa de Jesús: aventura humana y sagrada de una mujer* (Salamanca, Spain: Sígueme, 2001), 30–31.

Now we can understand the true evangelical revolution that her reforms initiated.[6] In a church that looked much at lineage and "honor," Teresa, on accepting her nuns, did not ask for any lineage other than having God as father.[7] Thus she unmasked the lie and the false value of social honor by means of the total commitment to live in truth: "I'm saying that we should walk in truth before God and people in as many ways as possible. Especially, there should be no desire that others consider us better than we are. And in our works we should attribute to God what is His and to ourselves what is ours and strive to draw out the truth in everything. Thus, we shall have little esteem for this world, which is a complete lie and falsehood, and as such will not endure" (IC 6.10.6).

Teresa's family had resided in the city of Ávila since 1486. She was the daughter of the second marriage of Don Alonso Sánchez de Cepeda and Doña Beatriz de Ahumada, the fifth of twelve children, between Rodrigo and Lorenzo, her most beloved siblings. At the age of fourteen, after her mother died, she drew near to the Blessed Virgin, begging Mary to be her mother (L 1.7). Teresa's adolescence was difficult without the presence of her mother, and she let herself be influenced by the friendship of her cousins. When she got close to one of her cousins in particular, Teresa seemed to become vain and began to engage in worldly pursuits. Worried about this new influence on his daughter, Teresa's father decided to place her

---

6. Teresa of Jesus forms part of the renewal movement in the church whose goal was returning to a radically evangelical life. This movement arose as a response to the complacency and the search for honor and power that was alive in various religious orders, and which had no place in following Jesus.

7. "Will the great ones of the world, perhaps, be great before me? Or, are you to be esteemed for lineage or for virtue?" (ST 5).

for a time in the Monastery of the Augustinians of Our Lady of Grace in 1531. There she opened up to new friendships that began to shed light on her vocational road, but within a year she had to leave the monastery because of illness. On November 2, 1535, at age twenty, Teresa entered the Carmelite Monastery of the Incarnation where she would live until 1562. From age forty-seven to sixty-seven, Teresa lived her fully human and spiritual nature, as writer and founder, traveling the roads of Castile, La Mancha, and Andalusia.

Teresa's intellectual preparation, including her knowledge of Scripture, was uncommon among women of the nobility of those times.[8] From her *Book of the Foundations*, we also see that she was prudent and had an outstanding ability to manage funds.[9] She was interested in dowries as a means of helping maintain the convents and consulted the learned when she wanted to know if she should make the foundations with or without income; Teresa employed every type of economic strategy to free her nuns from being enslaved by the demands of the nobility, who in that era owned many of the monasteries.[10]

---

8. See Tomás Álvarez, *Cultura de mujer en el s. XVI. El caso de Santa Teresa* (Burgos, Spain: Monte Carmelo, 2006).

9. See Luis Ruiz Soler, *La personalidad económico-administrativa de la Santa Madre Teresa de Jesús* (Zarautz, Spain: Ed. Icharopena, 1970); José Álvarez Vázquez, *Trabajos, dineros y negocios. Teresa de Jesús y la economía del siglo XVI* (Madrid: Trotta, 2000).

10. The pressure from the nobility was inevitable, with the result that in the monasteries they founded or controlled, their families' offspring prevailed, both in numbers and in holding positions of authority. In effect, this resulted in a very real sellout of community life to the monopolies of the nobility, in such a way that "the great family names" were determining the monastic life of women. See Oro, "Reformas y observancias," 32–55.

Female monastic life had become a true aristocratic refuge. Many families of the nobility maneuvered to get their daughters and other female relatives elected as prioresses and abbesses, in order to assure them of a lifetime post. The "social rules of the world" dominated the monasteries, with divisions between nuns who were of the nobility and those who were not; these effectively became the servants of the noble sisters. Easy access to and the permanent presence of lay benefactors within monastic enclosures was seen as necessary and normal. The nuns at the Incarnation, for example, needed to foster good relations with benefactors in order to ensure sufficient income to maintain 180 to 200 nuns. This environment of allowing benefactors to live within the monastery or allowing the nuns to go out to see them was becoming a keynote of religious life, as Teresa portrays well with regard to the Incarnation, where she spent twenty-seven years of her life (see L 7.2–5). Therefore, in contrast, in the reformed Carmelites that she proposed, she did not want anyone to be called "Doña" (Lady), a title of respect, and she required that all be treated equally and all work, beginning with the superior. She thus eradicated titles and the differences of lineage,[11] in order to form communities where the fundamental rule was love and friendship: "In this house. . . . all must be friends, all must be loved, all must be held dear, all must be helped" (W 4.7).

The experience of her first years in the city of Ávila accustomed Teresa to dealing with nobles and knowing their rules. We know that she had no qualms about writing to the king, preventing the princess of Eboli from tyrannizing the nuns,

---

11. See Alison Weber, "Spiritual Administration: Gender and Discernment in the Carmelite Reform," *Sixteenth Century Journal* 31, no. 1 (2000): 123–46.

attending the duchess of Alba, or in living some months with the noble lady of Toledo, Doña Luisa de la Cerda. She spoke the same way with everyone: businessmen (the majority of them Jewish converts who supported her foundations economically), mule drivers, construction workers, students, bishops, and the great "learned ones."[12]

In summary, taking note of her family and cultural roots, the church, and social conditioning in which sixteenth-century women lived (unavoidable aspects of the environment in which Teresa was raised) permits us a greater knowledge and understanding of Teresa's mission. We gain another perspective of her life, her writings, her relationships and conflicts, her internal and external suffering, and all the struggles and difficulties that accompanied her throughout the whole length of her sixty-seven years of life.

A Poor Little Woman Like Myself

Teresa experienced for herself the reality of what it meant for women to be disregarded. She relates an episode that is "to be much wept over" (F 20.3). A couple, upset because they had had a daughter instead of a son, neglected the newborn, leaving her near death: "On the third day after her birth they left their baby girl alone and forgot about her for the entire day, from morning until night, as though she mattered little to them. . . . When at night, a woman who was taking care of the baby came and realized what was going on, she hastened to see if the child was dead" (F 20.4). Teresa analyzes this situation, showing how different are the ways of God:

---

12. See Ismael Bengoechea, *Teresa y las Gentes* (Cádiz, Spain: Padres Carmelitas Descalzos, 1982).

Certainly, it is something to be much wept over that human beings do not know what is best for them and are totally ignorant of the judgments of God and of the great blessings that can come to them through daughters or of the great sufferings that can come from sons. It doesn't seem they want to leave this matter to the One who creates their children and understands everything, but they kill themselves over what should be making them happy. . . . Oh, God help me! How differently will we understand these ignorances on the day when the truth about all things shall be understood. And how many fathers and mothers will be seen going to hell because they had sons and also how many will be seen in heaven because of their daughters. (F 20.3)

Obviously, the reception and acceptance of Teresa's work was affected by an environment so hostile to women. It's more than a little surprising to the modern reader to learn that, on several occasions, friends, confessors, and members of the order refer to Teresa as "male." Disparaging her female gender in this way effectively devalued her feminine nature as a person capable of virtue, wisdom, and learning.

In the society in which Teresa lived, the concept of being a woman was incompatible with that of being strong. A woman was known to be weak, frail, and insignificant, and those characteristics made her a woman. This stereotype formed part of what was considered culturally as "the feminine identity." Some values, such as spirit, strength, and the ability to reason, were associated with being male. We find ourselves facing a cultural concept of gender. That is, consciously or unconsciously, a concept of the identity of a woman or of a man and the role that she or he should play had been formed. That a woman could have strength simply didn't correspond to the cultural concept of what was understood by being woman, even though there certainly were many strong women in that era.

On publishing Teresa's biography, Francisco Ribera, a Jesuit priest who knew and loved her, verifies that in the thinking of the sixteenth century, there was a "cultural significance of gender" that functioned as an ideology of what it means to be male or female.[13] He refers to dealing with the mystical experiences of Teresa: "Someone will say that, oh well, she was a woman, and that one does not have to pay much attention to the revelations of women,"[14] and he explains later, "Those who conquer their passions with force and subject them to God, have to be called men, and men who let themselves be conquered by them are women. It does not consist in the difference of body, but in the strength of the soul. . . . So we don't pay attention

---

13. When he asked permission of the general, Father Rodolfo Acquaviva, to publish Teresa's writings, Ribera received the following reply: "I received from Your Reverence the letter in which you asked for two things: first, that I give you license to print the life of Teresa of Jesus, a Carmelite nun. It seems to me that this subject is more suitable to some friar of her order, and that I should not give it to someone of the Society, nor should we occupy ourselves in writing lives of *beatified women*; besides this, *it does not suit the authority of your person* and the ministry that you exercise that Your Reverence now deliberately put yourself to print this life, *given that you have brought to light works of greater importance*, and I hope that you will do more; and so I am inclined that you leave this to someone else to do." León Lopetegui, "Censura de la Orden de la Vida de Teresa de Jesús, por Francisco de Ribera, SJ," *Manresa* 16 (1944): 264 (emphasis added). Thanks be to God, the love and admiration that Ribera professed for Teresa of Jesus led him to persist, and he obtained the permission after three years of lengthy dialogue.

14. Francisco Ribera, *La Vida de la Madre Teresa de Jesús: Fundadora de las descalzas y descalzos carmelitas* (Madrid: Edibesa, 2005), 88.

to revelations of women, that is to say of weak people, overcome by their passions; but one must pay attention to those of
a woman more masculine than many great men, so dynamic
and brave, and to those that resemble her."[15]

The stereotype of woman persists when he says, "We
don't pay attention to revelations of women," and he subverts
Teresa's gender, asserting that "those who conquer their passions with force and subject them to God have to be called
men," because Teresa as woman was not capable of conquer-
ing her passions and subjecting them to God. With this reasoning, Ribera attains two things. First, he gives value to her
work, inasmuch as he was dealing with not just a woman who
had revelations but "a woman manlier than many men." He
also distinguishes strength as a quality "of man" that is found
in men and women, intuiting perhaps that both sexes have
certain feminine and masculine characteristics—even without going out of his cultural concept that impeded his seeing these qualities as feminine. Ribera shows us the dominant
mentality and the common thinking that could not accept
that a woman had revelations. Thus it was better to treat her
as "male," because if she were treated as female, they would
have to ignore her revelations.

In the sermons and celebrations of the festivals of beatification and canonization of St. Teresa, the idea of her having perfected her nature and, therefore, having transformed
herself into a male is repeated: "This woman ceased to be a
woman, *restoring herself to the state of a man to her greater glory
than if she had been [a man] from the beginning, for she corrected nature with her virtue*, returning to the bone from which

---

15. Ribera, 88.

she sprang."[16] To be a woman signified having an imperfect nature;[17] and to be a man, a perfect one. Thomas Aquinas, having assimilated the mentality of the age, attributes the birth of a female, clearly second order, to some accident or failure, perhaps even a humid wind: "Only by considering the nature of the individual is it seen that the woman is something defective and of the second order. So the power that operates in the seed of the man tends to produce something equal to itself, perfect in its masculinity; but the procreation of a female is the result of the weakness of this active power or of some inadequacy of material, or of some change provoked by external influences, like the south wind, for example, that is humid, as Aristotle tells us."[18]

Given this prevailing view of woman, Teresa had to handle it carefully in order to obtain any recognition, especially because the censors, the first to receive her writings, were always male. In the past, expressions such as "I realized I was a woman and wretched" (W 1.2) and "everything can be harmful to those as weak as we women are" (W Prol 3) were considered as referring to humility and even to a certain sense of humiliation. At present, however, literary critics are suspicious of this excessive repetition of self-disparagement for being female: "just being a woman is enough to have my wings fall

---

16. *Relación sencilla y fiel de las Fiestas* (1627), cited in Ahlgren, *Teresa of Ávila*, 165 (emphasis added).

17. Biologically, the woman was considered only a nutritive container, and the origin of life was thought to come from the man. This was believed until 1827, when Karl Ernst von Baer discovered the eggs of mammals, offering the first scientific description of the participation of the woman. *Gran Enciclopedia Universal* (Madrid: Espasa Calpe, 2004), 153.

18. Francisco Barbado Viejo, *Suma Teológica de Santo Tomas de Aquino*, vol. 1 (Madrid: Editorial Católica, 1957), q. 92, a.1, ad. 1.

off" (L 10.8); "woman and wretched as well" (L 10.8); "she is a woman; and not a good, but a wretched one" (L 18.4); and "a useless little woman as helpless as I" (F 2.4).[19] They concur that the use of these expressions has a marked intentionality of "capturing benevolently," considering that this repetitive form is a literary strategy to gain slack in an adverse situation and procure the empathy of the readers.[20] Alison Weber has treated it as a feminine rhetoric in which the author strategically anticipates the possible objections of her readers and repudiates them in advance.[21]

The censors had two major objections to her writings: first, because she is a woman, and second, because it seemed to them that she was not virtuous enough to have received such graces. "They consider this person lacking in humility, especially if she is a woman, and point out that she desires to teach the one from whom she should be learning" (L 20.25). It has been suggested that Teresa professed weakness as an intentional strategy to answer the anticipated criticism from the Holy Office.[22] She was racially Jewish, spiritual, female, and what is worse, an ardent reader of spiritual books that were subsequently forbidden. In her were united all the

19. See Weber, *Teresa of Ávila*; Ahlgren, *Teresa of Ávila*; and Marcos, *Mística y Subversiva*.

20. "For the opposition of good men to a little woman, wretched, weak and fearful like myself, seems to be nothing when described in so few words" (L 28.18).

21. Weber, in *Teresa of Ávila*, makes an interesting study in which she analyzes the use that Teresa makes of expressions of apparent disvaluing of woman and all that this signified in her time. This aspect has been studied from a literary perspective, identifying the strategies that Teresa used as a writer, in Marcos, *Mística y Subversiva*.

22. See Marcos, *Mística y Subversiva*, 36–37.

characteristics that the Inquisition considered suspect. What automatically appeared as the greatest obstacle, however, was that of being a woman. It is possible that she made use of the symbolic inferiority of women in order to subtly gain the favor of the reader: "And a complete nothing am I" (L 31.24); "if I were a person who had authority for writing" (L 6.8); and "I'm not worth anything" (L 39.13).

This Teresian strategy is considered one of the most subversive elements of her work,[23] united on occasion with a very fine irony: "In the case of *a poor little woman like myself, weak and with hardly any fortitude,* it seems to me fitting that God lead me with gifts, as He now does, so that I might be able to suffer some trials He has desired me to bear. But when I see servants of God, *men of prominence, learning, and high intelligence* make so much fuss because God doesn't give them devotion . . . when they don't have devotion, they shouldn't weary themselves. They should understand that since His Majesty doesn't give it, it isn't necessary; and they should be masters of themselves" (L 11.14; emphasis added).

Certainly, these were hard times for a woman who was secure in her identity as a woman, but at the same time wanted to fulfill her profound apostolic call. This awareness of being woman appears as a tiresome repetition that she never stopped underscoring. For the mindset of the sixteenth century, it was unthinkable that a woman could write as Teresa did—for no reason other than that she was a woman. This theme is reiterated by the witnesses of the process of beatification and canonization, speaking of *The Interior Castle*: "Because it is so

---

23. See Marcos, *Mística y Subversiva.*

lofty that if it had not been by the revelation of God, it would have been impossible for her to have been able to write it even if she had more learning than what we can presume a woman had."[24] It was concluded that because she was a woman, she could not have written it, except by direct divine inspiration, without involving her own faculties.

In summary, because of the cultural concept of gender in the sixteenth century, authorities could not recognize the true nature of woman as equal to man, capable of sanctity, virtue, and learning. Perceiving Teresa as having an imperfect nature, one of second order, made it difficult for her human and religious richness, rooted in her feminine identity, to come to light.

Teresa as Founder: Between Desires of Freedom and Being Bound

In this part we will deal briefly with the sociocultural concept of the role of woman in the church and its consequences in Teresa's life. The conflict between the prevailing view and her own path became more evident when, after twenty-seven years of life in a monastic community, she undertook her work as an itinerant founder.

---

24. Silverio de Santa Teresa, ed., *Biblioteca Mística Carmelitana* (Burgos, Spain: Monte Carmelo, 1933, 1935), 3:61. See also the following quotes: "This mother Teresa was a woman without studies or letters, and so her style, method and art of writing must have been given by the Holy Spirit because it is not possible that in a woman without this intervention there be such an abundance of human learning" (ibid., 1:418). "Because it was impossible that a woman write the said books in such a superior and high style" (ibid., 3:263). "Well it is certain that the capacity for cleverness in a woman could not be stretched so far" (ibid., 3:68).

Around the age of forty, Teresa began to have mystical experiences that changed the direction of her life. Her profound experience of the love of God could not be contained, and she was filled with a burning desire to communicate it to the world, a desire that was frustrated by the situation: "It [Teresa's soul] would want to enter into the midst of the world to try to play a part in getting even one soul to praise God more. *A woman in this stage of prayer is distressed by the natural hindrance there is to her entering the world, and she has great envy of those who have the freedom to cry out and spread the news abroad about who this great God of hosts is.* Oh, poor little butterfly, bound with so many chains which do not let you fly where you would like!" (IC 6.6.3–4).

Envying those who can freely proclaim who this great God is, Teresa longed to shout, to announce the kingdom, to preach, but she was hindered by being a woman. She communicated it to Father García de Toledo, for whom she had written *The Book of Her Life*: "Your Reverence ought to cry out these truths since God has taken from me freedom to do so" (L 27.13). She struggled continually between the great desire to proclaim the kingdom and the little freedom that she found to do it: "Oh, who will cry out for You, to tell everyone how faithful You are to Your friends!" (L 25.17).

Father Jerome Gracián, Teresa's confidant and ally, explained the great force of her apostolic zeal and her desire to liberate herself from the lack of courage, which prevented what her interior spirit was crying out for: "A thousand times she was sighing to be able to have liberty, talents, and offices that men have, in order to bring souls to God, preaching, confessing and converting Gentiles even to spilling blood for Christ; and never did she pressure me to do anything other than to preach always, giving me much advice and counsel for this."[25]

Paradoxically, it was this very frustration that moved her to initiate the Carmelite reform. As a woman, she could not go out to preach publicly, but since she could no longer contain her desires to serve the Lord, she decided to dedicate herself to contemplative prayer. She wanted to announce the God of mercy, even if only "pushing from the rear guard," and she dedicated herself, together with other sisters, to pray for those who preach.

Two historical events shook her internally and drove her to make this decision: the division in the church and the lack of evangelization of the "Indians" in the Americas:

> At that time news reached me of the harm being done in France and of the havoc the Lutherans had caused . . . The news distressed me greatly, and, as though I could do something or were something, I cried to the Lord and begged Him that I might remedy so much evil. It seemed to me that I would have given a thousand lives to save one soul out of the many that were being lost there. I realized I was a woman and wretched and incapable of doing any of the useful things I desired to do in the service of the Lord. All my longing was and still is that since He has so many enemies and so few friends that these few friends be good ones. As a result I resolved to do the little that was in my power; that is, to follow the evangelical counsels as perfectly as I could and strive that these few persons who live

---

25. Francisco Ribera, *Scholias y adiciones . . . a la vida de la Madre Teresa*, cited by Tomás Álvarez, ed., *Obras completas de Santa Teresa* (Burgos, Spain: Monte Carmelo, 2002), F 1.7, n 8.

here do the same. I did this trusting in the great goodness of God, who never fails to help anyone who is determined to give up everything for Him. (W 1.2)

In a letter to Gracián on December 13, 1576, she shared, "Every day I am learning more about the fruit of prayer and the value before God of a soul that for God's honor alone seeks help for others. Believe me, *mi padre*, I think the desire is being accomplished for which these monasteries were founded, which was to pray to God to help those who struggle for his honor and service, since we women count for nothing" (Ltr 162.5).

The other historical event that moved her was having news of the "Indians" and wanting to go to them to announce the kingdom:

A Franciscan friar happened to come to see me . . . who had the same desires for the good of souls as I, *but he was able to transfer them into deeds for which I envied him greatly.* He had recently come back from the Indies. He began to tell me about the many millions of souls that were being lost there for want of Christian instruction. . . . I was so grief-stricken over the loss of so many souls, that I couldn't contain myself. . . . I cried out to the Lord, begging Him that He give me the means *to be able to do something to win some souls to His service,* since the devil was carrying away so many, and that my prayer would do some good, *since I wasn't able to do anything else.* I was very envious of those who for love of our Lord were able to be engaged in winning souls, though they might suffer a thousand deaths. (F 1.7; emphasis added)

Teresa was longing for a freedom that had been taken from her (L 27.13). The contrast between the need to cry out the abundance of God and the feeling of being "bound with so many chains" (IC 4.6.3) that kept her from doing so was a constant drama, a tension that breaks out repeatedly in her writings. As we know, Teresa managed the situation as best she could, without ceasing to do what the love of God and the desire to save souls inspired her to do. Making the foundations involved leaving the cloister, dealing with muleskinners, noblewomen, bishops, and students, and this won her the reprimand of the nuncio: "Restless woman, wanderer, disobedient and obstinate, who in the name of devotion invented bad doctrines, going outside the cloister, against the order of the Council of Trent and prelates, teaching as a master, against what Saint Paul taught, ordering that women should not teach."[26]

She was meditating on these things in prayer, wondering if they could be right (those who thought her making foundations was evil), when she heard from the Lord: "Tell them they shouldn't follow just one part of Scripture but that they should look at other parts, and ask them if they can by chance tie my hands" (ST 15).

They did not tie the Lord's hands, nor those of Teresa, who had profound and difficult experiences of the sociocultural conditioning of the sixteenth-century church. Notwithstanding this adverse situation for women, she founded

---

26. Francisco de Santa María, "Reforma de los descalzos," I, IV, c.30, n. 4661, in Tomás Álvarez, ed., *Diccionario de Santa Teresa* (Burgos, Spain: Monte Carmelo, 2002), 1149.

seventeen monasteries throughout all of Spain, traveling in wagons or on mule back, enduring the tremendous heat of Seville, encountering bulls in Medina del Campo, and dealing with floods in Burgos. Although the religious woman of her time was forbidden to leave the cloister, to preach, or to teach—for these activities were outside of what was considered the role of a holy woman—nothing stopped Teresa's indomitable, restless spirit.

She Writes as She Speaks: Teacher of Life

Teresa's work as a writer began in 1562, at age forty-seven. Her first book, *The Book of Her Life*,[27] was born of two objectives: the need to proclaim "the mercies received" and obedience to her confessors, who had ordered her to write. The style is "confessional," influenced by Teresa's reading of St. Augustine, and had as intended readers and witnesses the group of theologians, friends, and confessors who wanted to help her discern her personal experiences in prayer.[28] Father Domingo Bañez, her confessor and censor, gave his approval before the Inquisition judges, but as he didn't approve of its publication,

---

27. *The Book of Her Life* was preceded by two works that have not been passed down to us: a short story of chivalry, which she wrote in her adolescence, and one or more "general confessions" that she handed in to her demanding advisers, who wanted to discern the good or bad spirit of her prayer. In the spring of 1562, she undertook the first redaction of *The Book of Her Life*, which she revised three years later. Only this second redaction has reached us. See Álvarez, *Obras Completas*, 10.

28. Those identified in the first redaction are Gaspar Daza (diocesan priest), Baltasar Álvarez (Jesuit), Pedro Ibáñez (Dominican), and Francisco de Salcedo (gentleman of Ávila); and for the second redaction these priests sent her to García de Toledo and Domingo Bañez, both Dominicans. See Álvarez, *Obras completas*, 31.

he handed it in to the Inquisition in 1575.[29] Although Teresa tried to get the book back many times, she died without seeing it again.

The Index of Valdés (named for its Inquisition-appointed author, Fernando Valdés y Salas), published in 1559, prohibited the reading of the Bible and many spiritual books and works on mysticism, as well as their publication in the vernacular. Because this limited possible sources of formation for her nuns, Teresa saw the need to write something to help them. In 1566, at age fifty-one, prompted by their pleas and their love for her, she wrote the first edition of *The Way of Perfection*, usually called "Códice Escorial" (draft manuscript, so named because it is now in the royal library at El Escorial). She later drafted *The Book of the Foundations*, beginning in 1573, and *The Interior Castle* in 1577, when she was sixty-two. In addition, she composed several short works, such as *The Soliloquies, Meditations on the Song of Songs, Poetry*, and an abundant collection of several thousand letters, of which only 455 have been recovered.[30] In 1579, after corrections, censures, and deletions by her censors, she prepared the second edition of *The Way of Perfection*, called the manuscript of Valladolid, which was published in 1583, some months after her death. The history of the redaction and appearance

---

29. "Because she had many revelations and visions, which are always much to be feared, especially in women . . . yet it was very certain that as much as is humanly possible she was trying not to deceive; so because of her transparency, her good intentions and good works deserve to be regarded favorably." Domingo Bañez, "Censura en el autógrafo de la Vida de Sta. Teresa," in *Obras Completas de Santa Teresa*, ed. Efrén de la Madre De Dios and Otger Steggink (Madrid: Editorial Católica, 1977), 190–91.

30. Tomás Álvarez, *Cartas Santa Teresa* (Burgos, Spain: Monte Carmelo, 1979), 31.

of each one of her books is quite an adventure that involves censorship, secret copies made by the nuns, analysis, and condemnation. Father Diego de Yanguas even ordered *Meditations on the Song of Songs* to be burned, but we still have it today—thanks to secret copies made by one of the nuns.[31]

The literary style of Teresa's writings makes her communication empathetic, colloquial, close, and familiar.[32] Following the characteristics of her expression and writing, one can unravel some characteristics of her femininity, such as empathy and the ability to establish connections.[33]

As a good teacher and mother, she uses all types of strategies and techniques to obtain a concrete objective, to entice and win the reader: "His Majesty knows besides obeying [my superiors by writing] it is my intention to attract souls to so high a blessing" (L 18.8). She utilizes every possible strategy in order to make herself understood by her audience and to "capture their good will" without paying much attention to the "nonsense" of her style that resulted from concentrating on her goal. This form of writing gave her a surprising logic that enchants and captivates more than any planned and well-organized discourse could have.

---

31. "Fr. Diego de Yanguas told this witness that that Mother Superior had written a book about the Song of Songs, and it seemed to him that it was not right that a woman write about Scripture and told her so, and she was so prompt in obedience to the opinion of her confessor that she burned it immediately." Testimonio de María de San José Gracián, in Silverio de Santa Teresa, *Biblioteca Mística Carmelitana*, 1:320.

32. I refer the reader to the work by the Carmelite Juan Antonio Marcos, *Mística y Subversiva* (Madrid: Editorial de Espiritualidad, 2001). Writing from the viewpoint of philology, Marcos applies the most modern linguistic theories and unravels the expressive mechanisms of Teresa of Jesus. The organization of her message reflects well the rhythm of her thinking.

33. See note 7 of the Introduction in this text.

Her form of communication was totally innovative among the spiritual books of the sixteenth century, because most of their authors were men such as John of the Cross, conditioned by philosophical terms.[34] Teresa of Jesus was not educated, so she did not rely on terms that would make her restrict the lived experience within an orthodox and conceptual language. Yet she communicated the highest levels of mysticism with an "unpretentious elegance," in the words of Father Luis de León, in a way that broke the stereotypical rhetoric.[35] Luis was himself an outstanding mystic of the age, and one of Teresa's first readers and critics. Teresa freely explored images, symbols, and comparisons of all types, enabling the reader to understand better what she was trying to communicate.[36]

Her literary style is colloquial. That is, she wrote as she spoke: "So, I shall be speaking to them [her nuns] while I write" (IC Prol 4). When we read Teresa we are present at a long conversation maintained with her nuns, or with the

---

34. St. John of the Cross as "lettered" uses philosophic categories to express his mystical experiences in a doctrinal body inspired by Pseudo-Dionysius the Areopagite, with a certain Platonism. He writes about the experiences of prayer—with these categories, within the framework of orthodoxy that was required in that historical era. See Juan Martín Velasco, *El fenómeno místico. Estudio comparado* (Madrid: Editorial Trotta, 1999), 367–98.

35. Luis de León, "Carta Dedicatoria a la Madre Priora Ana de Jesús y Religiosas Carmelitas Descalzas del Monasterio de Madrid," in *Los Libros de la Madre Teresa de Jesús Fundadora de los Monasterios de Monjas y Frailes Carmelitas Descalzos de la Primera Regla* (Madrid: la Imprenta Real, 1597).

36. "I shall have to make use of some comparison, although I should like to excuse myself from this because I am a woman and write simply what they ordered me to write. But these spiritual matters for anyone who like myself has not gone through studies are so difficult to explain. I shall have to find some mode of explaining myself, and it may be less often that I hit upon a good comparison" (L 11.6). See note in Álvarez, *Obras completas*, 109.

readers, in which, in the midst of joviality and freshness, there is a feeling of family and friendship. She thus creates empathy and connection, writing as she continues thinking aloud, almost without ever erasing or crossing out. Curiously, if she wants to correct something, she does it in the thread of the conversation and rewrites or reformulates: "*But as I said elsewhere*, the reason why in this kind of prayer . . . (I am referring to the kind of prayer this dwelling place began with, *for I have joined the prayer of recollection, which I should have mentioned first, with this one.* The prayer of recollection is much less intense than the prayer of spiritual delight from God that I mentioned. But it is the beginning through which one goes to the other; for in the prayer of recollection, meditation, or the work of the intellect, must not be set aside)" (IC 4.3.8; emphasis added).

We find innumerable citations of this type: "They said I was trying to make myself out to be a saint and was inventing novelties. . . . So without any fault on their part they accused me. *I don't say that only the nuns did this*, but there were other persons as well. They revealed truths to me because You permitted this, Lord" (L 19.8; emphasis added).

Her colloquial style reveals the empathy that she shows for the reader and for the people she relates to. She captures their attention, involving them and disposing them to an encounter with God.[37] This force of attraction and connection permits her to enter into a profound resonance and communication with whoever reads her. Through her writing she

---

37. "One who had met with her often assured me that no one talked to her who didn't get lost in her . . . that in her interaction, her orderliness and good appearance, the discretion of her speech, and the gentleness moderated by honesty made her so appealing that both the profane and the

creates a relationship that can move people, provoking them to change. Sharing her deeper experiences, Teresa becomes an excellent teacher of life. She has moved countless numbers of readers to an encounter with God throughout more than four hundred years. Among them we note Blessed Charles de Foucauld, whose vocational decision was influenced by Teresa, and who subsequently continued reading *The Book of Her Life* in the desert.[38] In 1921 another great woman, Edith Stein, now herself a canonized saint, was totally captivated by reading *The Book of Her Life* and was unable to stop until she finished, confessing, "This is the truth!"[39]

Teresa's way of relating as a woman is shown in her empathy, her closeness, her imagination, and her ability to connect with the people she interacts with and with her readers. Her concrete and practical thinking in dealing with the highest degrees of mysticism reveals that her experience of life is developed in everyday events. Teresa comes to systematize her lived experience in a doctrinal way in her later writings, especially in *The Interior Castle*, where the images, comparisons, and metaphors are taken not from theories but from life.

---

holy . . . stayed as prisoners, captivated by her." Luis de León, *De la vida, muerte, virtudes y milagros de la Santa Madre Teresa de Jesús* (Salamanca, Spain: Universidad de Salamanca, 1991), 112.

38. Jean Francois Six, *Vie de Charles de Foucauld* (Paris: Editions du Seuil, 1962), 46–49.

39. Edith Stein, *Il castello dell'anima: riflessioni sul Castello interiore di s. Teresa d'Ávila* (Florence, Italy: OCD, 1981), 17–21.

Between "Authority and Daring": Her Teaching

Teresa of Jesus is a master at understanding life and is recognized particularly as a teacher of prayer. We know that a sixteenth-century woman was prohibited from teaching; she was not thought capable and therefore had no authority.[40] "It [the soul] would want to cry out in order to make known how deceived they are—sometimes it even does so, and a thousand persecutions rain down upon its head. They consider this person lacking in humility, especially if she is a woman, and point out that she desires to teach the one from whom she should be learning. As a result they condemn this soul—and with reason—because they don't know the loving impulse that moves it. For at times the soul can't help but disillusion—nor endure not disillusioning—those whom it loves" (L 20.25).

When we read Teresa's own words, we understand that the experiences she lived enkindled a fire within her, so that she could not remain silent; they impelled her to communicate the graces that she had received and experienced. Since she could not preach, she founded monasteries to pray; as her nuns did not have a place to learn, she wrote for them, based on the authority that her experience had given her: "I believe there are few who have arrived at the experience of so many things" (L 40.8).

---

40. We recall the quote of Luis de León: "Nature did not make good, honest women for the study of science, nor for managing difficult matters, but for only one simple and domestic office, so it limited their understanding and consequently fixed their words and reasoning powers." Félix García, *Obras completas castellanas de Fray Luis de León* (Madrid: Biblioteca de Autores Cristianos, 1991), 320.

Each one of her pages is laced with appeals to her own experience as a source of personal authority. Julian of Ávila, the chaplain for Teresa's foundations, explains in the processes of beatification, "All that she says is known from experience. And it is well understood that if among so many who write from learning, there is one who writes from experience, then there is a tremendous advantage of that one over the others."[41]

To better understand the source of Teresa's authority, we need to remember the context. As we noted previously, two fundamental currents can be distinguished in the ecclesiastical environment. On one side were "the learned," who were well prepared and educated, basing their teaching on theology and philosophy. Although Teresa was not so educated as they were, she valued them and followed their criteria: "Also, learning is a great thing because *learned men teach and enlighten us who know little*; and, when brought before the truths of Sacred Scripture, we do what we ought. May God deliver us from foolish devotions" (L 13.16; emphasis added).[42]

There were also "the spirituals," who appealed to the experience of God, inviting all to live what they preached. Some of the learned were also among these spirituals. With the division of the church in Germany and the appearance of the Alumbrados, however, an air of suspicion of the lettered toward the spirituals was developing in Spain. A campaign

---

41. Silverio de Santa Teresa, *Biblioteca Mística Carmelitana*, 1:222

42. This citation, like others, echoes the tensions between theologians and spiritual people, and the conflicting opinions of whether or not the learned who are not spiritual can direct those who are spiritual people of prayer. She herself had received a letter from Peter of Alcántara (a spiritual Franciscan) in which he emphasizes that "perfection in life is not a matter for anyone except those who live it." Silverio de Santa Teresa, *Biblioteca Mística Carmelitana*, 2:125–26.

against the spirituals as "suspected of Alumbradism" was unleashed, encouraging people to use only vocal prayer and carrying caution to an extreme, all but prohibiting mental prayer for women.

When Teresa wrote *The Way of Perfection* and *The Interior Castle* to teach her nuns the way of prayer, she was convinced of the power that arose from the profound encounter with God in mental prayer. She knew by experience that true vocal prayer must be preceded by mental prayer; if not, it is only moving the lips.[43] "Now, I tell you, sisters, if before you begin your vocal prayer you do the great deal that must be done in order to understand these two points well, you will be spending a good amount of time in mental prayer" (W 22.3). To motivate her nuns to mental prayer, she tries to take away their fears and suspicions. "I don't understand what they fear who fear to begin the practice of mental prayer. I don't know what they are afraid of. The devil is doing his task well of making the truth seem evil" (L 8.7). She knew what was being said and what her nuns had surely heard from the learned and from confessors: "You will hear some persons frequently making objections: 'there are dangers'; 'so-and-so went astray by such means'; 'this other one was deceived'; 'another who prayed a great deal fell away'; 'it's harmful to virtue'; 'it's not for women, for they will be susceptible to illusions'; 'it's better they stick to their sewing'; 'they don't need these delicacies'; 'the Our Father and the Hail Mary are sufficient'" (W 21.2).

She knew the great benefits that come to a soul with a deep relationship with God, for she had lived it, experienced

---

43. "A prayer in which a person is not aware of whom he is speaking to, what he is asking, who it is who is asking and of whom, I do not call prayer however much the lips move" (IC 1.1.7).

it. Her authority and teaching arose not only from this lived experience but also from her many sufferings, which were for her a crucible in the search for truth in her long process of prayer. She tells in *The Book of Her Life* how she came under suspicion of Alumbradism because of some revelations she had had. In her heart, however, she was sure of her fidelity to the church and of her love of the Scriptures, and this gave her a surprising freedom of spirit:

> Likewise the devil began striving here through one person and another to make it known that I had received some revelation about this work [the foundation of San José in Ávila, the first monastery]. Some persons came to me with great fear to tell me we were in trouble and that it could happen that others might accuse me of something and report me to the Inquisitors. This amused me and made me laugh, for I never had any fear of such a possibility. If anyone were to see that I went against the slightest ceremony of the church in a matter of faith, I myself knew well that I would die a thousand deaths for the faith or for any truth of Sacred Scripture. And I said they shouldn't be afraid about these possible accusations; that it would be pretty bad for my soul if there were something in it of the sort that I should have to fear the Inquisition; that I thought that if I did have something to fear I'd go myself to seek out the Inquisitors; and that if I were accused, the Lord would free me, and I would be the one to gain. (L 33.5)

She wrote this passage after having endured great conflicts with her confessors in the consultations that she had with them over the experiences of prayer. Her love and fidelity to the Scriptures and to the church were not just words; she had proved her faithfulness in innumerable sufferings, for she was seeking the truth and was afraid of being deceived. Her confessors told her that what she was living in prayer was demonic: "It seemed so certain to them that I had a devil that some persons wanted to exorcise me" (L 29.4). And they told her that she was being fooled like the Alumbrados. They investigated her confessor, questioning him: "I knew that they told him to be careful of me, that he shouldn't let the devil deceive him by anything I told him; they brought up examples to him of other persons. All of this made me anxious. I feared that I would have no one who would hear my confession, but that all would run from me. I did nothing but weep" (L 28.14).

And when she tried to explain what had happened to her, her profound experience became more incomprehensible: "They asked me some things; I answered plainly and carelessly. At once they supposed that I wanted to teach them and that I thought I was wise. It would all get back to my confessor, for certainly they [the learned] desired my good; and he would again scold me. This lasted for a long time, in which I was afflicted on all sides" (L 28.17–18).

Teresa felt that "the learned" did not understand what had happened in her soul because they had not lived anything similar. "I saw that no one understood me; I knew this very clearly" (L 30.1). But this burden was greatly lifted the first time she spoke to Friar Peter of Alcántara,[44] a man who understood her because he himself had lived her experience:

---

44. "He took the greatest pity on me. He told me that one of the worst trials on earth was the one I had suffered (which is contradiction on the part of good men)" (L 30.6).

"This holy man enlightened me about everything and explained it to me, and he told me not to be grieved but that I should praise God and be so certain that all was from His Spirit that with the exception of the faith nothing could for me be truer or more believable" (L 30.5). Teresa confirms the necessity of having a teacher and experience in the ways of the Spirit: "However, experience and a spiritual master are necessary because once the soul has reached those boundaries many things occur about which it is necessary to have someone to talk to. . . . There are many more women than men to whom the Lord grants these favors. This I heard from the saintly Friar Peter of Alcántara—and I too have observed it—who said that women make much more progress along this path than men do. He gave excellent reasons for this, all in favor of women; but there's no need to mention them here" (L 40.8).

A Woman Teach?

Teresa's experience and teaching were refined through trial by fire: She was accused seven times by the Inquisition.[45] And in the background of all the accusations was simply—and lamentably—that she was teaching ideas of the Alumbrados,

---

45. The analysis of each one of the accusations, as well as the errors of perception and the doctrinal ones of the inquisitors, were analyzed extensively in Enrique Llamas, "Santa Teresa de Jesús ante la Inquisición Española," *Ephemerides Carmeliticae* 13 (1962): 518–65; Enrique Llamas, *Santa Teresa de Jesús y la Inquisición Española* (Madrid: Consejo Superior de Investigaciones Científicas, Instituto "Francisco Suarez," 1972); and Enrique Llamas, "Teresa de Jesús y los alumbrados. Hacia una revisión del 'alumbradismo' español del siglo XVI," in *Actas del Congreso Internacional Teresiano*, ed. Teófanes Egido, 137–67, vol. 1 (Salamanca, Spain: Universidad de Salamanca, 1983).

such as the practice of mental prayer. Her accusers were saying that the type of prayer that her nuns had in the monasteries was identical to that of the Alumbrados of Llerena and
that the doctrine of her books was the same as that professed
by those in Extremadura and Andalusia.[46] It seems that the
suffering caused by the confessors was an expression of the
general feeling against Teresa, which was later crystallized in
the accusations of the Inquisition. There were two principal causes of this suspicious attitude toward her: First, Teresa
continued to write spiritual books, in spite of the prohibi-
tion against similar books decreed by the Index of Valdés,
which was still in effect. Secondly, simply because she was
a woman, she was the object of the enormously exaggerated
misgivings, suspicions, and lack of confidence in women
during this period.[47]

Historical investigations increasingly demonstrate that
the theologians, and in particular the inquisitors, wanted to
prohibit women from mental prayer and deprive them of the

---

46. When the determining causes of the development of these accusations are analyzed, the historian Llamas notes, "Many events were motivated
by hidden causes; many characters were moved by secret lines of thought
that perhaps we will never manage to grasp." By this he refers specifically
to the people who backed the accusations of María del Corro in Seville and
of the princess of Eboli, who had been living as royalty in the monastery.
In order to free her nuns from their whims, Teresa took the nuns out of
the monastery, leaving the princess alone in her castle of Pastrana, probably
provoking the accusations that followed. See Llamas, "Teresa de Jesús y los
alumbrados," 147.

47. "Whoever underestimates or attempts to disvalue this problem perhaps ignores that climate of fear, suspicions, of opposition and lack of trust
toward a woman who was giving lessons on the spiritual life to the lettered who
believed themselves to have sole and total knowledge and authority regarding
spiritual matters." Llamas, "Teresa de Jesús y los alumbrados," 149–50.

fruits of the interior life.[48] The same Father Domingo Bañez, who had known Teresa for more than twenty years, and loved and admired her, says in the declarations for the process of beatification and canonization, "It wasn't fitting that this book [*The Book of Her Life*] be around in the public while she was living, but rather that it be guarded in the Holy Office until we see where this woman ends up."[49]

In the midst of so much suspicion and mistrust, we understand the complaint that Teresa lodged against the judges of this world, taking as her model Jesus, the just judge, and his attitude toward women. The following fragment of text in brackets was totally eliminated by the censors of the first edition of *The Way of Perfection* and recovered in the later investigations over the originals:

---

48. With the publication of *Malleus Maleficarum* in 1546, Heinrich Kramer and Jacob Sprenger further strengthened the antifeminist atmosphere, denigrating all that could signify the deviations of Alumbradism, chicanery, and illusions of women. This confirmed the theory in which it was affirmed that "fémina" (woman) is derived from "fe" (faith) and "minus," as if every woman, just by being a woman, had an innate proclivity to deceit and spiritual delusions. See Llamas, "Teresa de Jesús y los alumbrados," 152.

49. Silverio de Santa Teresa, *Biblioteca Mística Carmelitana*, 1:10. After Teresa's death, when her writings were first published in 1588 by Friar Luis de León, accusations began to spring up against her doctrine. Only one year later in 1589, the first accusation was made by Alonso de la Fuente, awakening a fierce persecution with four more accusers (supporters among them) that lasted until 1598. Bañez surely knew of the accusations of the Inquisition against Teresa. His testimony was made on October 16, 1591. Some of his statements, such as "although she was deceived she was not deceitful, for she was really looking for the light and showed both good and bad," and "until we see how this woman ends up," could have been motivated by fear and insecurity about possible implications for him for defending a woman accused by the Inquisition, considering that he held the first chair in theology at the University of Salamanca. It must be noted, however, that Teresa trusted him completely. Llamas, *Santa Teresa*, 402.

Nor did You, Lord, when You walked in the world, despise women; rather, *You always, with great compassion, helped them. [And You found as much love and more faith in them than You did in men.* Among them was Your most blessed Mother, and through her merits—and because we wear her habit—we merit what, because of our offenses, we do not deserve. Is it not enough, Lord, *that the world has intimidated us. . . .* [illegible] *so that we may not do anything worthwhile for You in public or dare speak some truths that we lament over in secret,* without Your also failing to hear so just a petition? I do not believe, Lord, that this could be true of Your goodness and justice, for You are a just judge and *not like those of the world. Since the world's judges are sons of Adam and all of them men, there is no virtue in women that they do not hold suspect.* Yes, indeed, the day will come, my King, when everyone will be known for what he is. I do not speak for myself, because the world already knows my wickedness—and I have rejoiced that this wickedness is known publicly—but because I see that *these are times in which it would be wrong to undervalue virtuous and strong souls, even though they are women].*" (W 3.7, emphasis added)[50]

Both her personal experiences of prayer with her confessors and her writings passed through the sieve of strong purification and discernment. Over the years, however, all of this has strengthened Teresa's teaching as a faithful woman. We

---

50. This text is from the autograph that was crossed out by the censors. The facsimile was edited in 1964, C. de Valladolid, and in 1984, C. Escorial. See Tomás Álvarez, "Santa Teresa y las mujeres en la Iglesia: Glosa al texto teresiano de Camino 3," *Monte Carmelo* 89 (1981): 121–32.

know that when she speaks to us of prayer and of life, she does so from what she has lived. In her writings we find abundant citations in which she confirms, "I shall say nothing about things of which I don't have much experience" (L 18.8). She appeals untiringly to it as the best argument of authority: "I have a great deal of experience in this matter, and I know that what I say is true, because I have considered it carefully" (L 11.15).

Teresa considers experience as the cornerstone necessary to teach others the way of prayer: "This love together with my age and *the experience I have* from living in some monasteries may help me in speaking of ordinary things to be more successful than learned men" (W Prol 3; emphasis added). Her experience becomes the source of her authority. Because of it, she boldly dares to assert that they should accept what she says to them: "Thus, until Your Reverence [to the Dominican García de Toledo] *finds someone with more experience than I*, and who knows better, you should keep to this opinion" (L 22.13; emphasis added). To her nuns she affirms with certainty and authority, "I am certain that great evils would be avoided if we were to understand that the whole matter lies not in guarding ourselves against men, but in guarding ourselves against displeasing You" (L 2.7). She knows that in order to guide others, experience serves more than theories, which are only thoughts. "*I have come to see by experience* that it is better, if they [the confessors] are virtuous and observant of holy customs, that they have little learning. For then they do not trust themselves without asking someone who knows, nor do I trust them" (L 5.3; emphasis added).

When Teresa decided to write in order to systematize her teaching and help her nuns in the way of prayer, she wisely anticipates the main objection they could raise to her writing about prayer: she is a woman. And she converts this weak point into a strength by referring to the advantage, namely, that her nuns would be able to comprehend her better: "The one who ordered me to write told me that the nuns in these monasteries . . . *would better understand the language used between women,* and that because of the love they bore me they would pay more attention to what I would tell them" (IC Prol 4; emphasis added). When she teaches them, she is clear and simple, and goes straight to the essential. She motivates them, knowing that if they learn it well, then they will not need more than Scripture to pray: "So it seems to me now that I should proceed by setting down some points here about the beginning, the means, and the end of prayer. I shall not take time to dwell on more sublime things. No one will be able to take from you these books (the Our Father and the Hail Mary), and if you are eager to learn you won't need anything else provided you are humble. I have always been fond of the words of the Gospels and found more recollection in them than in very cleverly written books" (W 21.3).

She was daring, bold, but also humble; she valued learning and was always counseled by the learned. She came to say, "A truly learned man has never misguided me" (L 5.3). On the other hand, she never stopped putting in their place those theologians who were supported only by reasoning: "I found so many disadvantages in having an income and saw it would be so great a cause of disquiet and even distraction that I did nothing else but dispute with learned men. I wrote about it to the Dominican religious who was helping us. He sent me two pages with objections and theology written on both sides on why I shouldn't do it. . . . I answered him that I didn't want to benefit from theology if it wasn't conducive to my following my vocation, my vow of poverty, and the counsels of Christ with total perfection, and that in this case he did me no favor with his learning" (L 35.4).

When she met with Peter of Alcántara, the opposite occurred: supported by experience, he counseled her to found her convents without income: "With this favorable opinion from one who could give the best opinion since he had known about poverty through wide experience, I made up my mind not to go looking for other opinions" (L 35.5).

Teresa's reform went to the most profound root of true renewal, and what is more, it was proposed by a woman criticized as incapable of living the Gospel because of her fragility and weakness. The provincial of the Dominicans of Spain expresses it well in the processes of beatification and canonization: "Teresa of Jesus and her nuns had shown the world that it is possible for women to follow evangelical perfection."[51]

As the years passed, Teresa of Jesus came to be considered a great saint throughout the whole world, popular for her doctrine and experience of God. The church, however, could not officially recognize her teaching. A cultural concept of gender was the fundamental reason: "obstat sexus" (gender impedes).[52] Finally, the Second Vatican Council brought the hour of "open windows," when a woman could be recognized as the subject of a special divine inspiration that illumines the whole of humanity. In 1970 Paul VI proclaimed

---

51. Silverio de Santa Teresa, *Biblioteca Mística Carmelitana*, 1:9.

52. See Antonio Royo Marín, *Doctoras de la Iglesia: Santa Teresa de Jesús, Santa Catalina de Siena y Santa Teresa de Lisieux* (Madrid: Biblioteca de Autores Cristianos, 2002).

her Doctor of the Universal Church. Currently through her writings, Teresa continues realizing what she had longed for: to "cry out for You, to tell everyone how faithful You are to Your friends!" (L 25.17).

In summary, Teresa was a spiritual woman who knew that mental prayer was necessary to encounter God. However, under the assumption that they might be easily fooled, women were asked to use only vocal prayer. Teresa fought boldly for the truth that she had come to know in her purification and discernment. The love of God and her apostolic zeal led her to overcome the limits that the culture of her time imposed on women, until she became a teacher of prayer for her sisters and for those who read her writings. The power of the experience of God kept on transforming her until, together with her sisters, she gave witness that by the road of prayer it is possible to live evangelical perfection.

3

Teresian Contributions to Gender and Culture

W e have seen how the cultural concept of gender is present in the mentality of the confessors, friends, inquisitors, and clerics who crop up repeatedly— to judge Teresa's writings, evaluate her experiences in prayer, identify her feminine virtues, give opinions about her apostolic activities, and describe how a woman should live a holy life. When we study Teresa's life from this perspective, we can see that cultural biases clearly had a marked influence on the definition of what it meant to be a man or a woman and on the role that each had to live out in society and in the church.

Culture and Human Dignity

Understanding gender from only these conscious or unconscious cultural concepts reduces the understanding of the person's totality as woman or man. It is necessary, however, to take into account the influence of gender in the formation of mental representations, since these concepts can function as a blind spot. This could confuse aspects that are merely historical-cultural with the announcement of the Good News and the way of living it, especially in relation to women and religious life today. Sadly, in the course of history this reductive understanding has had painful consequences, particularly in those that refer to the lack of respect for human dignity: ". . . every type of discrimination, whether social or cultural, whether based on sex, race, color, social condition, language or religion, is to be overcome and eradicated as contrary to God's intent. For in truth it must still be regretted that fundamental personal rights are still not being universally honored" (GS 29).

Since discrimination against women is contrary to the plan of God, we must therefore insist on a vision of the totality of the human person, according to which the formation of gender identity includes aspects that are cultural, relational, biological, corporal, religious, and spiritual. We need to unmask the cultural concepts, conscious or unconscious, that impede men and women from realizing the plan of God for each one, and which block our relationships as daughters and sons of God, sharing the common responsibility of caring for creation and constructing a world that is more just for all. Women and men have differences and similarities, and, by right and obligation, the common responsibility for our world belongs to both. Fulfilling this responsibility will be possible only in the measure in which women and men, the two faces of humanity, have the same possibilities of participation and making decisions in society.

A New Paradigm of Woman

Teresa of Jesus opened her life to the mystery of God and, through her fidelity to God, transcended many of the constrictions that society and culture imposed on her for being female. Clear and defined in her own identity, she lived in such a way that understanding her mission required a change of mentality about the concept of woman that predominated in the society and culture of the sixteenth century. We have commented on the difficulty that some of her contemporaries had in accepting certain aspects of her personality which did not fit into their cultural concept of woman, and so they preferred to refer to her as male.

In her own life, Teresa was actually presenting a new image of woman, one that originated from the most profound roots of human dignity. She knew and believed that God "created us [i.e., every man and woman] in His own image and likeness" (IC 1.1.1). This fundamental conviction was in reality the beginning of a common anthropological theology that went beyond gender. From this perspective, her whole reality as a woman, created by God in God's own image and likeness, and blessed with that identity, drove her to live a vocational call of transformation to the fullest, with all the sociohistorical consequences that this implied. Therefore she did not permit herself to be intimidated in the face of the persecutions that she suffered for being a woman; in spite of everything, she believed in her dignity as a child of God, called to a personal relationship with God, by means of mental prayer.

We can conclude that Teresa presented a new paradigm of what it meant to be a woman. Her writings and witness continued to challenge the church for four centuries, until she was proclaimed Doctor of the Universal Church. Then it was recognized publicly and officially that woman is equal to man on the religious and spiritual level, and that the conditioning that leads one to recognize this truth or not comes from historical-cultural values. This historical and cultural assessment of woman had impeded the understanding and valuing of Teresa of Jesus as a woman, with the characteristics proper to her feminine nature. Identifying this problem helps us to see the validity and usefulness of this investigation and the richness that it can offer to the reader.

Teresa as a Relational Woman

We have seen that Teresa's literary style and strategies allowed her great capacity for connection and empathy to show through. These gifts, markedly feminine, made her way of prayer possible and also determined how she perceived her relationship with God, the apostolic mission, and community life in the Carmelite reform.

For Teresa, prayer is a special kind of friendship. "For mental prayer in my opinion is . . . an intimate sharing between friends; it means taking time frequently to be alone with Him who we know loves us" (L 8.5). Some conditions are necessary in order to have this friendship: "In order that love be true and the friendship endure, the wills of the friends must be in accord. . . . And if you do not yet love Him as He loves you because You have not reached the degree of conformity with His will, you will endure this pain of spending a long while with one who is so different from you when you see how much it benefits you to possess His friendship and how much He loves you" (L 8.5).

Friendship asks us to tolerate differences until we become like the true Friend. Teresa actually lays the foundations for community life in her reformed monasteries on this experience of relationship: "In this house . . . all must be friends, all must be loved, all must be held dear, all must be helped" (W 4.7). She was inviting them to be "staunch friends of God . . . to sustain the weak" (L 15.5). This human aspect of Teresa has clearly marked the characteristics of the contemplative Carmelite life.

In Teresa of Jesus all the riches of this empathetic and connected relational aspect can be seen in her way of being with Christ and in prayer. These feminine qualities are the foundation for fully living the love of God and of our sisters and brothers.

PART 2

The Interior Castle

4

Characteristics of the Book

The process behind the development of *The Interior Castle* is described in detail in the historical note by Tomás Álvarez and Antonio Más in the reproduction of the facsimile of *The Interior Castle*, according to the autograph preserved in the Monastery of the Discalced Carmelites in Seville.[1] I present a brief synthesis of that note here, to help the reader understand the process of its conception.

Gestation

We know that when Teresa sat down to write in 1577, she was initially thinking of redoing her *Life*, written in 1562, and still in the hands of the Inquisition; she planned to add some of her experiences of the twelve years since its completion (see IC Prol 2). She had learned that the bishop of Ávila had a copy and was thinking to integrate everything in the same

---

1. Tomás Álvarez and Antonio Más, *Reproducción en facsímil del Castillo Interior* (Burgos, Spain: Monte Carmelo, 1990).

book. In a letter to her brother Lorenzo, she noted, "I wrote to the bishop [Don Álvaro de Mendoza] to ask him to send the book [*her Life*], for perhaps I will be stirred to finish it by writing about what the Lord has given me since. Or another large one could be written," (Ltr 177.19, January 17, 1577).

She became exhausted by excessive work, however, and the doctors forbade her to write in her own hand; she could do so only by means of a scribe. In February 1577 she suffered from "noise and weakness in [her] head," and she wrote to Father Ambrose Mariano that she was afraid of remaining incapable of doing anything (Ltr 185, February 28, 1577). At the end of May, recovered somewhat from exhaustion, she met with Father Jerome Gracián, her confidant and spiritual director, in the Toledo Carmel. He was on his way from Seville to Madrid, and she was following the instruction given by the general chapter of the order in Piacenza of 1575 "that you choose a house where you will always stay and not make any more foundations." She had also been told by the provincial superior that she was becoming an apostate and would be excommunicated if she were not cloistered once and for all in one of her monasteries.[2] Gracián refers to it in the marginal notes of the biography of St. Teresa:

> What happened with regard to the book of the *Dwelling Places* [*The Interior Castle*] is that while I was superior and speaking with her once in Toledo of many things concerning her spirit, she said to me: "Oh, how well this point was described in the book about my life which is in the Inquisition!" I answered, "Since we cannot have it, recall what

---

2. See Maximiliano Herráiz, ed., *Obras completas de Santa Teresa de Jesús* (Salamanca, Spain: Ediciones Sígueme, 1997), 576.

you can and other things and write another book, but put down the doctrine in a general way without naming the one to whom the things you mentioned there happened." And thus I ordered her to write this book of the *Dwelling Places*. (Collected Works, Vol. II, p. 263)

Birth

In the prologue and epilogue of *The Interior Castle*, Teresa explains when and how she began to write the book. Gracián's mandate, together with her confessor's urging, moves Teresa to action, even though she finds herself little disposed to it. She feels uninspired, and the "noise and heaviness of head" continue: "Not many things that I have been ordered to do under obedience have been as difficult for me as is this present task of writing about prayer. First, it doesn't seem the Lord is giving me either the spirit or the desire to undertake the work. Second, I have been experiencing now for three months such great noise and weakness in my head that I've found it a hardship even to write concerning necessary business matters" (IC Prol 1).

She wanted to have written it before, but she had not been able to, and now obedience compelled her to do it.[3] So in the Carmelite Monastery of St. Joseph in Toledo, she began to write on the feast of the Holy Trinity in the year 1577; according to the note of Teresian scholar Father Tomás Álvarez, the feast was celebrated on June 2 that year.[4] In the

---

3. "But knowing that the strength given by obedience usually lessens the difficulties of things that seem impossible, I resolved to carry out the task very willingly, even though my human nature seems greatly distressed" (IC Prol 1).

4. Tomás Álvarez, ed., *Obras completas de Santa Teresa* (Burgos, Spain: Monte Carmelo, 2002), 661.

epilogue she says that she finished on November 29, 1577, at the monastery of St. Joseph in Ávila (IC Epil 5). It had taken six months, including a long interruption of almost five months.[5] In fifteen days—alternating with the responsibilities of communal and personal prayer, correspondence, and other duties—she wrote the first, second, and third dwelling places, and finished the first chapter of the fourth, totaling in all twenty-six folios, or fifty-two full pages.[6]

The death of the nuncio, Nicolas Ormaneto, was followed by the appointment of Bishop Felipe Sega, who was openly opposed to Teresa. This threatened danger, even the undoing of the Carmelite reform, and Teresa prepared to return to Ávila. Between these interruptions, travels, and startling events, she composed the next five chapters, for nineteen more folios. And while Teresa was in the final stages of her writing, another storm was unleashed in the Monastery of the Incarnation, which she had just left: Teresa had been named prioress, but against the wishes (and without the vote) of the nuns, setting off a furor. Yet a few months later, in a little corner of the Monastery of St. Joseph, in the cold of November in Ávila, she finished the book with one stroke, without being able to reread what she had written in June. Starting at the fourth chapter of the fifth dwelling places, she wrote the last sixteen chapters of the twenty-seven

---

5. "It seems to me you have a desire to see what this little dove is doing and where it rests since as was explained it rests neither in spiritual delights (*gustos*) nor in earthly consolations (*contentos*). Its flight is higher, and I cannot satisfy your desire until the last dwelling place. May it please God that I then remember or have the time to write of this. About five months have passed since I began, and because my head is in no condition to read over what I've written, everything will have to continue on without order, and perhaps some things will be said twice" (IC 5.4.1).

6. See Álvarez, *Obras completas*, 648.

that comprise the work, from folio 46 to 110.[7] In these difficult conditions, she completed one of the loftiest works of Christian mysticism in scarcely more than two months.

She had wanted to hand over *The Interior Castle* to "the holy Friar Juan" (John of the Cross) so that he could read it, but four days after she finished it, he was taken prisoner.[8] Teresa worked to exhaustion on John's behalf, resorting not only to her terrible antagonist, the princess of Eboli, but also to King Philip II, trying to free John from prison. In the epilogue of her work she comments to us that her lack of inspiration and ailments have disappeared. "Although when I began writing this book that I am sending you I did so with the aversion I mentioned in the beginning, now that I am finished I admit the work has brought me much happiness, and I consider the labor, though I confess it was small, well spent" (IC Epil 1).

Later, between June 13 and July 6, 1580, in the visitors' parlor of the monastery of Segovia, Gracián, Teresa, and

---

7. Álvarez, 649.

8. Both secular and religious politics clashed with Teresa's reforms and the appointments of Carmelite superiors. The Carmelite chapter in Piacenza, Italy had decided on stricter rules regarding obedience, especially in Andalusia. John was now committed to the discalced way of life, and accompanied Teresa as her director and confessor at the Incarnation. When Teresa was about to leave the Incarnation, Nicolas Ormaneto, the papal nuncio, ordered him to stay, apparently because of his good work there. But the complicated tensions swirling around the state of authority and way of life soon led to his arrest by calced Carmelites in January, 1576. The nuncio soon had him released, but after the nuncio's death in June of 1577, John had no protection. He was soon captured and imprisoned in Toledo, where he refused to renounce his discalced way of life or his position at the Incarnation, which had come through legitimate authority. After nine months of suffering the terrible deprivation of imprisonment, John managed to escape. See Kieran Kavanaugh, OCD and Otilio Rodriguez, OCD, *The Collected Works of St. John of the Cross* (Washington, D.C.: ICS Publications, 1991), 17–19.

Diego de Yanguas (highly esteemed by Teresa as a theologian) met to simulate a tribunal judging the book. Gracián tells it this way: "Then Friar Diego and I read this book in her presence, with me arguing about many things in it, saying that they were offensive to pious ears, and Friar Diego answering my arguments, and she would say that we should take them out. And so we took some out, not because they were bad doctrine, but because they were lofty and difficult for many to understand. Because with a zeal as great as mine, she wanted to make sure that there would be nothing in her writings that anyone would stumble over."[9]

The book suffered innumerable misfortunes and interventions of all kinds throughout the next four centuries until 1962, when the restoration of the autograph was begun in the Instituto Alfonso Gallo de Roma, in order to prevent its further deterioration. Using the original, it was possible to authenticate Teresa's own changes in two pages added to the second redaction, in the seventh dwelling places, and in a place where she had sewn in a portion of paper that had been missing; these were added, together with her commentaries, some merely literary and others more doctrinal. Likewise, as Father Francisco Ribera had written in the first page of the autograph, the interference of "other hands" was identified;[10] on two occasions the editors had definitely changed the

---

9. Sérouet and Gracián, *Glanes*, 59–61.

10. "Many times in this book what the holy mother wrote is crossed out and other words are added or a gloss is put in the margin. And ordinarily it is poorly erased and what she had first written was better. And it will be seen that what is amended many times does not go well with what the holy mother says after that. And so the additions and glosses could well be omitted. And because I have read it and looked at everything carefully, it seemed to me to advise the reader to read it as the holy mother wrote it, who understood it and

meaning of the text. I refer those who are interested in learning more about this topic to the historical note in the Teresian facsimile. For the analysis of the text I have followed this restored edition of the autograph of *The Interior Castle*.

Organization

In order to provide some orientation for the reader, I think it will be helpful to look at the general structure of *The Interior Castle*.

It is organized in seven dwelling places, with a prologue and an epilogue. The distribution by chapters is as follows:

Dwelling Place	Number of chapters
Prologue	
1	2
2	1
3	2
4	3
5	4
6	11
7	4
Epilogue	

---

said it better, and leave out all the additions. Also, keep the erased words of the saint as if they had not been erased, unless they were amended or erased by her own hand, which happened very few times. And I beg, by charity, of whoever reads this book, that you reverence the words and letters made by that very saintly hand and try to understand it well; you will see that there is no need to amend it, and even though you may not understand it, believe that the one who wrote it knew better. The words cannot be corrected well if they do not completely convey the sense she intended; if they don't achieve that, what is very properly said will seem improper, and in this way the books will be corrupted and lost." Álvarez and Más, *Reproducción en facsímil*, 245.

At first glance, we can see that the distribution of the chapters is not proportional; the sixth dwelling places dominate, comprising more than 40 percent of the total number of chapters. Later we will see the significance of the relational aspects of these dwelling places, which are indeed among the most intense of the castle.

5

Dynamics and General Structure of *The Interior Castle*

The image of the castle functions more as a teaching method and as spiritual theology than as a symbol. With this image Teresa can simultaneously treat different aspects of the person's path toward the encounter with God. It combines the seven dwelling places that are the structure of the castle with other dynamic aspects, such as: the relationship with God; living from deep within the soul; and the dialectics between the interior and the exterior, between nature and grace, and among the body, senses, and faculties. The feminine aspect of Teresa's incarnated experience is perceived fundamentally in her way of experiencing and relating with herself, with God, and with others.

By way of introduction, in order to have a global vision and a better understanding of what will later be analyzed in detail in each dwelling place, we will now look at the dynamic and structural aspects of the castle.

Dynamic Aspects

The underlying thread woven throughout *The Interior Castle* is Teresa's relationship with God. It is her desire for union with him that drives her process of transformation. Teresa notes, however, that there are always forces in opposition to this desire, especially in the first dwelling places. The process is marked by a strong dialectic between the desire to enter into the castle and have a more intimate relationship with God and the desire to remain outside in the shadows, far from the light. To take steps toward one or the other side implies an option of drawing closer or moving away in the relationship with God. For practical considerations, we will treat these two aspects separately, even though they occur simultaneously and in an intimate interrelation.

Relational Dynamic

While many spiritual teachers had emphasized prayer in its rational and meditative aspects,[1] thus moving away from the corporeal,[2] Teresa, as a woman, reveals that the key to prayer

---

1. "It will also seem to you that anyone who enjoys such lofty things will no longer meditate on the mysteries of the most sacred humanity of our Lord Jesus Christ. Such a person would now be engaged entirely in loving. This is a matter I wrote about at length elsewhere [L 22]. They have contradicted me about it and said that I don't understand, because these are paths along which our Lord leads, and that when souls have already passed beyond the beginning stages it is better for them to deal with things concerning the divinity and flee from corporeal things. Nonetheless, they will not make me admit that such a road is a good one" (IC 6.7.5).

2. "I only wish to inform you that in order to profit by this path and ascend to the dwelling places we desire, the important thing is not to think much but to love much" (IC 4.1.7).

is an existential relationship with God; prayer is entering into a relationship, "an intimate sharing between friends; it means taking time frequently to be alone with Him who we know loves us" (L 8.5). This is the relationship that gives meaning to her life. Although it certainly requires specific times of personal encounter, it embraces all the dimensions of the person, and its effect is therefore extended to every moment of life. For Teresa it is an existential relationship incarnated in her very being as a woman. The intellectual knowledge of truth was very important to Teresa; this knowledge, however, did not come to her by instruction, nor by study, but through her relationship with the Lord, in whom she found the highest truth (see IC 6.10.7).

Entering the castle implies undertaking an existential relationship with God, and for Teresa the door to this relationship is prayer.[3] Even with prayer, however, the desire for change is not enough to sustain the process of transformation; a relationship of love that involves the whole person is necessary. Teresa shows this clearly in the experience narrated in *The Book of Her Life*, where she speaks of the love that the Friend bears for us; that love is what makes it possible to be in His presence, learning to love from who and what we are, without defensively hiding ourselves. In the castle this knowing oneself as loved by God begins with creation, since "He Himself says that He created us in His own image and likeness" (IC 1.1.1). Knowing herself beloved by God, together with the great desire for his friendship, gives her strength and helps her to bear being in front of the one who knows her: "In

---

3. "The door of entry to this castle is prayer and reflection" (IC 1.7).

order that love be true and the friendship endure, the wills of the friends must be in accord. The will of the Lord, it is already known, cannot be at fault; our will is vicious, sensual, and ungrateful. And if you do not yet love Him as He loves you because You have not reached the degree of conformity with His will,[4] you will endure this pain of spending a long while with one who is so different from you when you see how much it benefits you to possess His friendship and how much He loves you" (L 8.5).

This tension of enduring "this pain of spending a long while with one who is so different" and seeing her own truth before God,[5] allowing God to look at her, and herself to hear his calls, awakens dissatisfaction with the life that she had been living: "I see clearly the great mercy the Lord bestowed on me; for though I continued to associate with the world, I had the courage to practice prayer. I say courage, for I do not know what would require greater courage among all the things there are in the world than to betray the king and know that he knows it and yet never leave His presence. Though we are always in the presence of God, it seems to me the manner is different with those who practice prayer, for they are aware that He is looking at them" (L 8.2).

In the castle she systematizes all this experience narrated in *The Book of Her Life* and explains throughout all the dwelling places how she grows in knowing God and herself

---

4. "You cannot succeed in loving Him by yourself" (clarification by Tomás Álvarez, *Teresa de Jesús* [Burgos, Spain: Monte Carmelo, 2001], 88).

5. Teresa presents a relationship with God that implies maturation and growth in "otherness." To learn more about this aspect from the perspective of development, see Franco Imoda, *Sviluppo Umano, Psicología e Mistero* (Casale Monferrato, Italy: Piemme, 1993), 78–84.

through their personal encounter. In Teresa's model, realistic self-knowledge is essential for growth. In the first three dwelling places, it functions as the catalyst to begin to change and embark on the road; and in the last four, it is the key to discerning the relationship in prayer, the mystical graces, and possible deceptions. Realistically basing life on the truth of her own self is what helps her to escape her own dynamics of self-deception, creating the possibility of changing, growing, appropriating what she lives, and thus taking responsibility for her own life.

From Teresa's perspective, this self-knowledge includes the senses, the affections, the body, and all her feminine psychology. Beginning with the fourth dwelling places, the senses, the faculties and the body change from being enemies one must struggle with; they become allies that participate fully in the relational experience with God. For Teresa, self-knowledge, rather than "spiritualized" flights from reality, starts from the concrete experience of life, which includes all of her psycho-sexual being as a woman. Contrary to the dualistic soul-body theories of the sixteenth century, Teresa manifests "in the lived experience" a surprising integration and unity of body and soul, although it seems that she herself expresses a kind of dualism, as will be seen in the process of integration of the human—which in Teresa is feminine—and the divine.

Her relationship with God continues to change throughout the process. In the first dwelling places she is the one who actively seeks, while God communicates through mediations. In the measure in which she advances, however, Teresa reveals to us a God who intervenes directly in the relationship, and who furthermore makes himself subject to her in the relationship.[6] There is a progressive communication of his presence that begins to expand the heart according to God's measure until arriving at an integration of the human and divine that has its culmination in the spiritual marriage with Christ. "Such a person walks continually in an admirable way with Christ, our Lord, in whom the divine and the human are joined, and who is always that person's companion" (IC 6.7.9).[7]

In summary, from her feminine being, Teresa defines prayer as a relationship with the Lord Jesus, involving her whole being more and more. Beginning with the fourth dwelling places, her own body, together with her feelings, affect, and faculties, participate more deeply in the relational experience, as a whole that is involved without being compartmentalized. As the relationship deepens, the human integration of her being a woman is also realized. Throughout the process she uses her skills of empathy and connection in order to be in front of the One who knows us and loves us. Self-knowledge in truth and from the relationship is a key point for growth, discernment, and knowledge of the highest truth.

---

6. "He is the one who submits, and He wants you to be the lady with authority to rule; He submits to your will" (W 26.4). This theme is presented well in Pedro Cerezo Galán, "La Experiencia de la Subjetividad en Teresa de Jesús," in *La Recepción de los Místicos*, ed. Salvador Ros García, 171–204 (Salamanca, Spain: Universidad Pontífica, 1997).

7. See Juan Martín Velasco, "Búscame en tí—Búscate en mí. La correlación entre el descubrimiento del hombre y descubrimiento de Dios en Santa Teresa," in *Actas del Congreso Internacional Teresiano*, ed. Teófanes Egido, 800–834, vol. 2 (Salamanca, Spain: Universidad de Salamanca, 1983), 825.

Teresa's Search for the Truth

Teresa experienced a *dialectic* throughout her life: the opposition of internal forces that she considered to be present in the process of the dwelling places.[8] In the first three dwelling places, the struggle between living in the exterior or the interior, in the darkness or in the light (represented as Christ who is the sun, who illumines the castle), is very evident.[9] In the following dwelling places, the tension is between living in the natural and living in the supernatural (see IC 4.1.4), between action with Martha and contemplation with Mary (see IC 7.1.10; L 22.8), until arriving at that integration in which Martha and Mary are united (see IC 7.4.12).

For Teresa, entering into the first dwelling places implies bringing faith to life through experience. To stay in the exterior is to stay with the knowledge of what faith tells us but without having experience of it: "It is a shame and unfortunate that through our own fault, we don't understand ourselves or know who we are . . . when we do not strive to know who we are, but limit ourselves to considering only roughly these bodies. Because we have heard and because faith tells us so, we know we have souls" (IC 1.1.2).

This way of faith consists in knowing ourselves and knowing God, discovering that we are inhabited by the great King in the center of the soul: "You mustn't think of these dwelling places in such a way that each one would follow in file

---

8. I understand the concept of dialectic as an inherent movement to human motivation and as a consequence of the person's desire to transcend oneself. See Luigi M. Rulla, *Anthropology of the Christian Vocation* (Rome: Gregorian University Press, 1986), 150.

9. "The sun that is in this royal chamber shines in all parts" (IC 1.2.8).

after the other; but turn your eyes toward the center, which is the room or royal chamber where the King stays, and think of how a palmetto has many leaves surrounding and covering the tasty part that can be eaten. So here, surrounding this center room are many other rooms; and the same holds true for those above. The things of the soul must always be considered as plentiful, spacious, and large" (IC 1.2.8).

She invited her nuns and all who read her book to experience what we say we believe by faith: we are inhabited by God. This implies welcoming the life that is within the self. As a woman, she needed to pass from a merely rational knowledge to knowing from the heart—having an experience of God while God experiences her.[10]

In *The Interior Castle*, Teresa has elaborated the anxiety and the interior conflict generated by this struggle on the way of faith. In *The Book of Her Life* she manifested it more openly and told how, from her childhood, she had searched for God and longed for transcendence: "The Lord was pleased to impress upon me in childhood the way of truth" (L 1.4). On entering adolescence, however, and later in the monastery, for almost twenty years, she struggled on a tempestuous sea in which she experienced strong tension between her profound desire to find God and her attachment to sensual pastimes and joys: "I should say that it is one of the most painful lives, I think, that one can imagine; for neither did I enjoy God nor did I find happiness in the world. When I was experiencing the enjoyments of the world, I felt sorrow when I recalled

---

10. We recall the well-known quotes of Pascal: "We know the truth not only by reason but also through the heart" (Blaise Pascal, *Pascal's Pensées* [New York: E. P. Dutton, 1958], n. 110); and "The heart has its reasons that reason knows nothing of" (ibid., n. 477).

what I owed to God. When I was with God, my attachments to the world disturbed me" (L 8.2).[11]

Here we have the problem of Teresa's personality described: emotional attachments, pleasures, friendships, and the danger of a mediocre life. She perceived an interior division in herself as a deep-rooted conflict, shown in the struggle between letting herself be carried along and living outwardly, or choosing to live inwardly. At the root of Teresa's conflict was her need for communication and affective relations— with people or with God. This was the great suffering of her life that was sapping all her energy.

> I was living an extremely burdensome life, because in prayer I understood more clearly my faults. On the one hand God was calling me; on the other hand I was following the world. All the things of God made me happy; those of the world held me bound. It seems I desired to harmonize these two contraries—so inimical to one another— such as are the spiritual life and sensory joys, pleasures, and pastimes. In prayer I was having great trouble, for my spirit was not proceeding as lord but as slave. And so I was not able to shut myself within myself (which was my whole manner of procedure in prayer); instead, I shut within myself a thousand vanities. (L 7.17)

---

11. "And would that I had the permission to tell of the many times I failed God during this period by not seeking support from this strong pillar of prayer. I voyaged on this tempestuous sea for almost twenty years with these fallings and risings and this evil—since I fell again—and in a life so beneath perfection that I paid almost no attention to venial sins. And mortal sins, although I feared them, I did not fear them as I should have since I did not turn away from the dangers" (L 8.1–2).

How was she to confront this tension? The truth, impressed in her heart from childhood, together with the pangs of dissatisfaction, impels her to find an adequate solution.[12] The anxiety created by the tension of trying to reconcile these two opposing forces moves her toward a road of owning her truth while trusting in God,[13] a road of liberation, of fidelity and surrender by means of her relationship with Christ: "Well, my soul now was tired; and in spite of its desire, my wretched habits would not allow it rest. It happened to me that one day entering the oratory I saw a statue they had borrowed for a certain feast to be celebrated in the house. It represented the much wounded Christ and was very devotional so that beholding it I was utterly distressed in seeing Him that way, for it well represented what He suffered for us" (L 9.1).

She connected her sensitivity as a woman, her feelings of empathy, compassion, and love on seeing "the much wounded Christ," with her profound spirit of faith. From that moment on, she made a qualitative leap in her long process of searching. Now she wanted to be totally at one with the truth of God from the depths of her soul and with no uncertainty.

---

12. Terrance G. Walsh, "Writing Anxiety in Teresa's Interior Castle," *Theological Studies* 56 (1995): 251–75. This author speaks of the presence of anxiety throughout Teresa's life, as was shown in her struggle to be with God, as well as in the fears and worries that she surely lived amid the accusations of possible Alumbradism and her marginalization and persecution for being a woman and daring to write. All of this created an internal state that pushed her to keep trying to overcome these situations.

13. "For I was very distrustful of myself and placed all my trust in God. I think I said then that I would not rise from there until He granted what I was begging Him for. I believe certainly this was beneficial to me, because from that time I went on improving" (L 9.3).

The Teresian struggle still continues throughout the course of the dwelling places, but the tone changes in each one. When Teresa begins to open her heart to Christ in the fifth dwelling places, she takes her first steps in real love and the dialectic is now between a love centered in the self and a love "without much self-interest," a love more freely given. In the sixth dwelling places, which are those of purification, the struggle shifts to that between being fixed on herself and others, and abandoning herself totally to God, whom she discovers as the ultimate truth. The conflict is unleashed precisely by questioning her relationship with God. As we have already seen, women were being advised to use only vocal prayer, and Teresa, seeking the truth, was afraid of being deceived. To this was added the insecurity that she felt "for not being learned," together with the little credibility that was given to her for being a woman. We can hypothesize that she lived with great anxiety and anguish, in great fear of being deceived. Influenced by the cultural concept of women held by society in her time, her self-concept must have also been affected. In many passages we can imagine her questions: Is the relationship I have with God real? Are these experiences of mine just the fruit of my imagination? Additionally, the doubts and accusations of confessors increased her fear of being an Alumbrada (see chapter 1 in this text):

> Let us begin with the torment one meets with from a confessor who is so discreet and has so little experience that there is nothing he is sure of: he fears everything and finds in everything something to doubt because he sees these unusual experiences. He becomes especially doubtful if he notices some imperfection in a soul that has them, for it seems to such confessors that the ones to whom God grants these favors

must be angels—but that is impossible as long as they are in this body. Everything is immediately condemned as from the devil or melancholy. . . . But the poor soul that walks with the same fear and goes to its confessor as to its judge, and is condemned by him, cannot help but be deeply tormented and disturbed. Only the one who has passed through this will understand what a great torment it is . . . the trial becomes something almost unbearable. (IC 6.1.8.)[14]

The conflict just described between her desire to live in the truth and her fear of being deceived was the impetus that thrust Teresa into an enormous detachment from herself and led her to discern her experiences against possible mechanisms of self-deceit.[15] She trusted confidently that God

---

14. "I know of a person [she herself, as noted in the text] who had great fear that there would be no one who would hear her confession because of such gossip—so much gossip that there's no reason to go into it all here. And what is worse these things do not pass quickly, but go on throughout the person's whole life including the advice to others to avoid any dealings with such persons" (IC 6.1.4). "Well, with regard to going to my confessor, it is certain that what I am about to say happened many times. Although the confessors I dealt with and am dealing with at this time are very holy, they spoke harshly and scolded me; afterward when I told them, they themselves were surprised and told me that to refrain from doing so was not in their power. They tried hard not to do it again, for afterward they felt sorry and even scrupulous about having done this. But when I had similar trials of body and soul and they were determined to comfort me with compassion, they were unable to do so. They didn't say any evil words—I mean that would offend God—but said the most unpleasant allowable in a confessor. They must have meant to mortify me; and although at other times I was glad and ready to suffer such mortification, during the time of this experience everything was a torment to me" (L 30.13).

15. "That this favor is no fancy is very clear. Although at other times the soul may strive to experience this favor, it will not be able to counterfeit one. . . . There's no basis for thinking it is caused by melancholy, because melancholy does not produce or fabricate its fancies save in the imagination.

communicated with her in her condition of being a woman (see IC 6.6.4). The purification of this crucible yielded a profound mastery of life and of prayer that was not easily conquered by difficulties.[16]

In summary, in Teresa the woman, her tendency toward relationship and connection is a double-edged sword in her process of encountering God. In the first dwelling places, it functioned as a movement against her desire to have an experience of God. The immediacy of the concrete in relationships and friendships acted as an impediment to entering within herself and initiating an experience of faith in solitude. This created a strong interior conflict. Once she was touched by grace, however, she was reoriented toward God, passing through a sifting process in her relations with God and with others. The struggle lived in each dwelling place is about deepening this relationship, which leads her toward a "decentered" love in the fifth; a trust that allows her to abandon herself totally in the arms of the Father and die to herself in the sixth; and to the fullness of her relationship with Christ in the spiritual marriage in the seventh.

This favor proceeds from the interior part of the soul" (IC 6.2.7). "About locutions, all the kinds I mentioned can be from God or from the devil or from one's own imagination" (IC 6.3.4). "I gave him a summary account of my life and manner of proceeding in prayer as clearly as I knew how. I always tried to speak with complete clarity and truthfulness to those with whom I conversed about my soul. I desired that they know even about any first stirrings, and I accused myself of matter that was doubtful and questionable with arguments against myself. Thus without any duplicity of covering over I discussed my soul with him" (L 30.3).

16. Teresa lived her own mystery in continuous confrontation, the difficulties functioning, with the help of God, as a possibility of growth. See Imoda, *Sviluppo*, 44.

Structural Aspects

Throughout *The Interior Castle* Teresa presents seven interrelated, dynamic stages of growth. When speaking of the structure of the castle, we refer to these seven stages of personal development that she describes throughout the life process.

To pass from one dwelling place to another implies taking a forward leap in the quality of relationship with God. The person is being transformed interiorly by this relationship, as is shown in different ways of functioning and behaving in each stage. Changes take place in every dwelling place, but there are two crucial points in the process. The first is in passing from the fourth mansions to the fifth, symbolized by the metaphor of the caterpillar transformed into a butterfly. This change is so strong that the person "doesn't recognize herself, nor her image."[17] We can say that her interior structure is qualitatively different, and she now achieves what she could not before.[18] The other qualitative leap that reconfigures her internally is the step from the sixth mansions to the seventh, where the divine and the human are integrated in the spiritual marriage.

We will call these crucial points of the process *structural changes*, inasmuch as the experience of relationship reconfigures the internal structure of the person, with consequences in

---

17. ". . . now that it understands through experience how the Lord helps and transforms a soul, for it doesn't recognize itself or its image" (IC 5.2.8).

18. "The weakness it previously seemed to have with regard to doing penance it now finds is its strength. Its attachment to relatives or friends or wealth (for neither its actions, nor its determination, nor its desire to withdraw were enough; rather, in its opinion, it was more attached to everything) is now so looked upon that it grieves when obliged to do what is necessary in this regard so as not to offend God" (IC 5.2.8).

behavior and in the mode of being and loving. These structural changes are normally progressive, so that each stage disposes one little by little for the structural changes that are consolidated in the fifth and in the seventh. There is always the possibility of rapid personal changes, however, given that "the Lord gives when He desires, as He desires, and to whom He desires" (IC 4.1.2).[19]

Teresa of Jesus uses the term "soul" to speak of the person being transformed. This word appears 275 times in the main text of *The Interior Castle* and 14 times in the introductions to the chapters. "We consider our soul to be like a castle made entirely out of a diamond or of very clear crystal, in which there are many rooms" (IC 1.1.1); a paradise for the one who lives in grace (see IC 1.1.1), it has great beauty, capacity, and value, but if you are in sin, it is something ugly (see IC 1.1–2). The soul enters within itself (see IC 1.1.5), and in the journey of prayer it can withdraw and hide away in a corner (see IC 1.2.8). Sometimes afraid to follow, the soul struggles with the voices of reason, faith, and the will (see IC 2.1.4). In *The Book of Her Life*, she tells us that the soul "grows" (see L 15.12), and in *The Interior Castle* she speaks of "an expansion or dilation of the soul" (IC 4.3.9). At the end of the process, it is the soul that sends messages and inspirations from the interior center to the inhabitants of the castle, so that the faculties, the senses, and all the members of the body will not be idle (see IC 7.4.10). At the end, the soul has characteristics of spaciousness, the spaciousness of a castle: a space of beauty;

---

19. Teresa considers that each person must make her or his own personal, original path. The fact that seven progressive stages are given does not exclude the unique pathway to growth that each individual experiences. She openly acknowledges that "God leads souls by many paths" (IC 6.7.12).

of value; of life and growth; of self-reference; of emotions, affects, and sensitivity; and of will, desires, and intelligence.

Teresa uses a great number of symbols for the soul: castle, palace, spirit, tree, building, house, wife, person, worm, silkworm, bee, butterfly, dove, wax, phoenix, straw, little boat, lightning, earth, bird, and hind. The synonyms that most share the characteristics of the soul, however, are the terms wife, the lady, person, and spirit, and the symbols of animals, such as those just mentioned.

Within the text the soul is sometimes the "poor soul" that suffers damaging influence in the first dwelling places and at other times the "great soul" that is ready to fight wind and sea in order to advance and enter the seventh dwelling place; in other moments, it is the silkworm that works on its house-tomb (the chrysalis) or the transformed butterfly that cannot find anywhere to settle in this world. It is also "the lady," who is found with her Spouse in the center of the castle. Each synonym of the soul has symbolic content that highlights the characteristics of changes in the relationship and in the person.

Throughout the process the soul is recognized as the same, from the first to the seventh mansions; it has the same identity, it lives a process of continuous growth, but as it goes on changing, it is being restructured in such a way that it does not know itself.[20] This characteristic of continuity in personal identity throughout the process of growth and transformation is essential to what we understand of the *self*.

---

20. "Truly I tell you that the soul doesn't recognize itself. Look at the difference there is between an ugly worm and a little white butterfly; that's what the difference is here" (IC 5.2.7).

In the *Diccionario de Santa Teresa* (Dictionary of Saint Teresa), the term *soul* is said to designate the spiritual component of the person.[21] The dictionary also affirms that "with great frequency the term soul designates the person herself."[22] At the beginning of the dwelling places Teresa uses the term soul in contrast to the term "body," which is the "setting" of the castle (IC 1.1.2), already forming part of the interior-exterior contrast that is given in the first dwelling places. In the last dwelling places, however, when the whole person has been involved in relationship and the body shares the spiritual experience, the author uses the term soul to also include the body.

There are some examples where we can clearly see how Teresa interchanges the term soul with the term person, utilizing a strategy to make a distinction within the same text, so that the soul as subject, that which experiences grace, becomes the person who narrates the lived experience. For example, in this citation we can see how Teresa begins referring to the grace that the soul receives: "As a result of this favor granted by God (to the soul)" (IC 6.9.7), and at the end of the paragraph she says, "How much more will the person fear this sight to whom the Lord has thus represented himself" (IC 6.9.7). Likewise, she moves from person to soul: "Perhaps He will respond as He did to a person who before a crucifix was reflecting with deep affliction that she had never had anything to give to God, or anything to give up for Him. The Crucified, Himself, in consoling her told her He had

---

21. See Tomás Álvarez, ed., *Diccionario de Santa Teresa* (Burgos, Spain: Monte Carmelo, 2002), 34–38.

22. Álvarez, 34.

given her all the sufferings and trials He had undergone in His Passion so that she could have them as her own to offer His Father. The comfort and enrichment was such that, according to what I have heard from her, she cannot forget the experience" (IC 6.5.6).

Mercedes Navarro Puerto has made a semantic study of the term "soul" in *The Interior Castle*.[23] She considers the term soul to be a self-referring description and takes this text as point of departure:

> Well, getting back to our beautiful and delightful cas-
> tle we must see how we can enter it. It seems I'm saying
> something foolish. For if this castle is the soul, clearly one
> doesn't have to enter it since it is within oneself. How fool-
> ish it would seem were we to tell someone to enter a room
> he is already in. But you must understand that there is a
> great difference in the ways one may be inside the castle.
> For there are many souls who are in the outer courtyard—
> which is where the guards stay—and don't care at all about
> entering the castle, nor do they know what lies within
> that most precious place, nor who is within, nor even how
> many rooms it has. You have already heard in some books
> on prayer that the soul is advised to enter within itself; well
> that's the very thing I'm advising. (IC 1.1.5)

Here Teresa presents a summary of what she is going to propose in the whole work. The soul enters within the self—although it is entering itself and is therefore considered a self-referring description. The objective of entering within oneself is to know

---

23. Mercedes Navarro Puerto, *Psicología y Mística. Las Moradas de Santa Teresa* (Madrid: Ed. San Pio X, 1992), 54–110.

oneself, in order to enter into relationship with God. In studying the frequency with which the word *soul* is used, Navarro Puerto also analyzes the use of various verbs and adjectives, and comes to distinguish the way the syntax of the soul functions. She concludes that the soul's most significant function is that of subject,[24] whether it is the subject of the narration or the object of the narration, as was seen in the discussion of the soul as person.

The soul-self-subject-person is presented fundamentally as a relational being. It knows itself, relates with itself, lives in relationship with others, and here is presented in its relationship with God. It is in this encounter where it is transformed. In the relational analysis and in the structural changes that Teresa presents to us in the dwelling places, we are going to use the Teresian term soul, bearing in mind that it deals with the subject, the person, and the self of Teresa—a woman's soul, with a feminine mode of feeling, relating, and realizing its mission.

With this analysis I have tried an approach of "coming and going," that is, from the text to us, and from us to the text, respecting as much as possible what Teresa presents to us and, at the same time, creating a bridge in order to be able to understand it from our perspective today. In spite of this approach, we must realize that there still must be a qualitative methodological leap since almost five centuries of history separate us from Teresa. The questions from which we begin the investigation of feminine identity and relationships were certainly never posed in this way in the sixteenth century. However, given that the narrator is a woman, we can make some

---

24. See Navarro Puerto, 84.

reasonable inferences about how her feminine dynamic enters into the mystical experience.

In summary, Teresa of Jesus proposes seven stages or states of growth for the soul. In this case, it is the soul of a woman who lives her experience from the feminine dimension involving her senses, body, faculties, and whole being. The seven stages of growth correspond to distinct qualities of relationship that reconfigure and restructure her, transforming her internally, with two crucial points: the fifth and the seventh dwelling places. In the book of *The Interior Castle*, when Teresa has understood and organized her personal experience of union with God, she invites everyone, men and women alike, to enter into the seventh dwelling places in order to enjoy a spousal relationship with God in a union that is both divine and human. As we shall see, this means that the spousal dimension of the church's relationship with God is a possibility for all the baptized.

6

The Feminine
Relational Dynamic

As we analyze the dwelling places through a feminine relational lens, we will look at the characteristics of the relationship in this process and see how this bond is formed. We will also try to differentiate the ways of living the relationship, since it is there, in subtle nuances that the "feminine" and "masculine" characteristics appear. The relationship with God will be seen as the source of the person's transformation.

The following four sections highlight the effects that emerge at various stages in the relationship, marking growth and maturation in relational characteristics.

Knowledge and Acceptance of Self:
Love That Is Pure Gratitude

The first three dwelling places form a stage of progressive growth in knowledge and acceptance of self, leading the person toward a relationship in which a love that stems from gratitude is awakened.

Images and Relationship with God

In this first stage of the relationship, God seems to be distant. The souls here can barely perceive the light from the interior,[1] and only with effort can they hear and distinguish the call of the Lord.[2] The images of God as powerful King (IC 1.1.1), His Majesty (IC 1.1.3), shining sun (IC 1.2.3), and Creator (IC 1.1.1) are found throughout the dwelling places,[3] but in this first stage they reflect a type of relationship in which God is far above the person. The images proposed for people who are beginning or who are still outside the castle are those of creatures (IC 1.1.1), "foul-smelling worms" (IC 1.1.3), "God's vassals" (IC 3.1.6), and "crippled souls" (IC 1.1.8)—and with them enter so many vermin that they cannot see the beauty of the castle or notice the light (IC 1.2.14). We could say that this stage deals with a relationship between Creator God and creature, between King and worm, between Majesty and vassal—a relationship that is clearly vertical and unequal.[4]

In the symbolism of the castle, the body is "the plainness of the diamond's setting or the outer wall of the castle" (IC 1.1.2). The body appears as the boundary between the exterior and the interior, between the external relationship and the internal

---

1. "Hardly any of the light coming from the King's royal chamber reaches these first dwelling places" (IC 1.2.14).

2. "Those who are in the first dwelling places are like deaf-mutes" (IC 2.1.2).

3. For this theme, the investigation of Ana Maria Rizzuto has made a valuable contribution. Ana Maria Rizzuto, *The Birth of the Living God* (Chicago: University of Chicago Press, 1979).

4. See Mary Frohlich, *The Intersubjectivity of the Mystic* (Atlanta: Scholars Press, 1993), 290–301. This author presents an interesting study on the intersubjective process in Teresa of Jesus.

one of silence and prayer. The soul (that has to enter within the self) and the body (as close to the castle) are both involved in this inside-outside dynamic. In spite of the dualist mentality of her time, Teresa perceives the body as significant in the relationship from the beginning of the process, and a progressive integration of the body, faculties, and feelings in the mystical experience is shown in the successive dwelling places.

Although the mentality of the age influenced Teresa, she was free of certain philosophical theorizing on the body-soul division. And more importantly from the perspective of this study, being a woman allowed her to live her affectivity and the integration with her own body more fully; it is widely accepted that women generally express their emotions more than men. We can also infer that because of their continuous experience with the menstrual cycle and the pain and other physical symptoms that accompany it every month, women are more in touch with their bodies. Furthermore, through the menstrual cycle, women also become aware of the body's connection with their emotions. All of this experience predisposes the woman to an earlier and greater integration of body and affectivity than might be the norm for a man.

In the three beginning dwelling places, the body, senses, and faculties are being drawn toward the outside, preventing the soul from entering into deeper mansions of the castle. They behave like enemies the soul has to struggle with in order to be reoriented toward God. Since they are turned toward the outside, the senses are disturbed and the faculties are blind (IC 1.2.4); they "don't have the strength God gave human nature in the beginning" (IC 1.2.12). In these three dwelling places their work consists in turning toward God and preparing themselves to enter into relationship with him.

Toward Growth in Love

For Teresa the person is so deeply inhabited by God that knowing and accepting oneself necessarily involves a relationship with him. This means that the process of personal knowledge is found in an anthropological perspective of transcendence. It is not a matter of looking only at our own wretchedness and remaining in it; that kind of self-knowledge, one that stays centered in the self, would make one "base and cowardly" (IC 1.2.11). Without a relationship with God, the soul remains incapable of recognizing its own great beauty and dignity. But the soul has been created in the image and likeness of God, and the Teresian proposal of "knowing oneself" holds that its own divine mystery is revealed in relationship with reference to God. It deals with an anthropological, theological and relational perspective: "The soul of the just person is nothing other than a paradise where the Lord says He finds His delight. So then, what do you think that abode will be like where a King so powerful, so wise, so pure, so full of all good things takes His delight? I don't find anything comparable to the magnificent beauty of a soul and its marvelous capacity. Indeed, our intellects, however keen, can hardly comprehend it, just as they cannot comprehend God; but He Himself says that He created us in His own image and likeness" (IC 1.1.1).

From the beginning of the relationship, Teresa, with her feminine awareness, perceives a bond of profound connection that begins with the creation of the human being, a bond of continuity with God by having been made in God's own "image and likeness."

Knowing another person implies approaching and welcoming the mystery of God in the other as well. Each one is the image of God, "His dwelling place;" and since we cannot totally know God, it would be futile to attempt to completely know any person,[5] where dwells this unfathomable mystery that is the living God: "The fount, the shining sun that is in the center of the soul, does not lose its beauty and splendor; it is always present in the soul, and nothing can take away its loveliness" (IC 1.2.3).[6] This manner of looking at oneself, as "inhabited by God" (see IC 1.2.3), involves a sense of interiority and of welcoming the life of God that inhabits the self; it is a profound feminine sense of oneself as the dwelling place of God.

At the same time there is distance between God and the creature, between God's state and ours. This distance increases when one is in sin, even though God still lives in the person because of creation (see IC 1.2.3). Teresa's feminine strategy for knowing God is not to emphasize the distance but rather to point out the connection with God, while seeing the contrast: "We shall never completely know ourselves if we don't strive to know God. By gazing at His grandeur, we get in touch with our own lowliness; by looking at His purity, we shall see our own filth; by pondering His humility, we shall see how far we are from being humble" (IC 1.2.9). This knowledge places the person in his or her own reality in front of the greatness of God.

For Teresa, self-knowledge in the light of God has its advantages. Interaction with him begins to unlock the understanding and move the will so that "our intellects and wills,

---

5. To believe that a human being is knowable by any of the sciences is to reduce his or her mystery, open to transcendence and the infinite.

6. When His Majesty says that it is made to his image, we can scarcely comprehend the great dignity and beauty of the soul (See IC 1.1.1).

dealing in turn with self now with God, become nobler and better prepared for every good" (IC 1.2.10). In the relationship, the person begins to be changed by God's communicating "a goodness so perfect and a mercy so immeasurable" (IC 1.1.3). She also considers this feminine principle of "contagion" in regard to relationships with good companions who can help one to enter within the castle.[7] Her relational perspective proposes coming to know God and being transformed by the loving relationship with him.

In spite of our poor human condition, Teresa experiences a gratuitous love by means of her relationship with God. She discovers this love through all that she has been freely given: life, dignity, beauty as the image of God, and redemption as a sinner saved by God;[8] all is gift of his love. However, in order to liberate us from a knowledge that traps us in our own misery,[9] she invites us to look at the love of God and the humility of Christ (see IC 1.2.11). This acceptance of our own condition in the face of the love of God freely given makes us recognize that "none of our good deeds has its principle from ourselves but from this fount in which the tree, symbolizing our souls, is planted and from this sun that gives warmth to our works" (IC 1.2.5). The fruit of this knowledge of the self

---

7. "It is a wonderful thing for a person to talk to those who speak about this interior castle, to draw near not only to those seen to be in these rooms where he is but to those known to have entered the ones closer to the center. Conversation with these latter will be a great help to him, and he can converse so much with them that they will bring him to where they are" (IC 2.1.6).

8. See IC 1.1.2. And, "Oh souls redeemed by the blood of Jesus Christ! Understand and take pity on yourselves! How is it possible that in realizing these things, you don't strive to remove the pitch from this crystal?" (IC 1.2.4).

9. "It would be disadvantageous for us never to get out of the mire of our miseries" (IC 1.2.10).

in humility is poverty of spirit, from which blossoms a profound gratitude and love.

Teresa explains the temptation involved in this process of knowledge and acceptance of the self in the third dwelling places. First, she summarizes the visible good effects of this state:

> Concerning souls that have entered the third dwelling places. . . . They long not to offend His Majesty, even guarding themselves against venial sins; they are fond of doing penance and setting aside periods for recollection; they spend their time well, practicing works of charity toward their neighbors; and are very balanced in their use of speech and dress and in the governing of their households—those who have them. Certainly, this is a state to be desired. And, in my opinion, there is no reason why entrance even into the final dwelling place should be denied these souls. (IC 3.1.5)

Teresa then explains the danger arising from these good works, namely, that after taking the first steps in virtue, these "well-ordered souls" may fall into the temptation of defending their own image. First of all, they may believe that they deserve entrance to the other dwelling places because of their virtuous works: "They cannot accept patiently that the door of entry to the place where our King dwells be closed to them who consider themselves His vassals" (IC 3.1.6). If they commit a fault, it is very difficult for them to recognize it as such, because "everything in their minds leads them to think they are suffering these things for God" (IC 3.2.2.), and "they would like everyone to live a life as well ordered as they do" (IC 3.2.5). Such people "canonize these feelings in their minds and would like others to do so" (IC 3.2.3). They are very much deceived, thinking that they have arrived at perfection because of their works, like the rich young man of the Gospel, whom Teresa uses as model of these dwelling places.

To accept that God's love is freely given implies recognizing that our works do not justify us before him. God's love is gratuitous, given to us in our weakness as sinners, not because we are just. It involves the humble recognition that the love we receive will awaken love (see L 10.4). This will make it possible for us to let go of security, to leave our nests, and to stay "unprotected" in order to embark on a new road: "If, like the young man in the Gospel, we turn our backs and go away sad when the Lord tells us what we must do to be perfect, what do you want His Majesty to do? For He must give the reward in conformity with the love we have for Him. And this love, daughters, must not be fabricated in our imaginations but proved by deeds. And don't think He needs our works; He needs the determination of our wills" (IC 3.1.7).

Until now "love has not yet reached the point of overwhelming reason" because the soul had not recognized the incredible free gift of so much love and good received" (IC 3.2.7). Only when the soul recognizes its need of redemption will it be liberated from its own slavery to the false image centered in self-justification by works. It is a matter of remaining in "nakedness and detachment from all worldly things" (IC 3.1.8), in order to set out on the way of wholeness, in an attitude of defenselessness and acceptance of one's own truth. This letting go would mark the birth of persons more true and genuine, whose acceptance of their own limits will make possible a greater integration of the self.[10] God welcomes the soul and at the same time leaves it free. He empowers the person to welcome and integrate aspects of its own poverty, history, and limits that were leading it to defend itself for fear of being rejected or losing its self-image.[11]

Relationship with Christ

We have focused on the relationship with God the Creator and King, but we can also ask about the relationship with Christ. We want to see how the person relates to Christ in these beginning dwelling places and how the feminine dynamic enters into the relationship. We know that Teresa considers this relationship from the viewpoint of the humanity of Christ and also that she values her own humanity embodied as female.[12]

---

10. In current thinking, the acceptance of one's own limits is a key step in the process of psychological maturation. The self becomes coherent inasmuch as it stops rejecting its own negative aspects, prolonging an irreconcilable split. The "cohesive" self recognizes its own truth and, thanks to the love perceived, goes on integrating positive and negative aspects of itself, the good and bad images of itself, as part of its own reality. This cohesion is brought about by factors that are cognitive, affective, volitional, and interpersonal, or by action. See Franco Imoda, *Sviluppo Umano, Psicología e Mistero* (Casale Monferrato, Italy: Piemme, 1993), 301–4.

11. In describing the stages of a person's maturation, Otto Kernberg explains this dynamic of resisting the realistic acceptance of the self due to the narcissistic wound. See Otto Kernberg, *Object Relations Theory and Clinical Psychoanalysis* (New York: Aronson, 1976); Italian translation, *Teoria della Relazione Oggettuale e Clinica Psicoanalitica* (Turin, Italy: Bollati Boringhiere, 1980), 179–210.

12. Teresa of Jesus inherited the spiritualist doctrine of her time, which counseled that in order to have a contemplative experience she had to distance herself from all that was corporal, and that included the humanity of Jesus. She confronted this problem at a practical and experiential level after she noticed that distancing herself from the humanity of Jesus Christ left her with

To help guard against distraction through the senses, she uses *la mirada*, the deep looking, or *gaze*.

In the first dwelling places she invites us to fix our eyes on Christ as a model of humility. She proposes this as a way of connecting with him: "So I say, daughters, that we should set our eyes on Christ, our Good, and on His saints. There we shall learn true humility" (IC 1.2.11). This aspect of gazing is central in Teresian contemplation: "I'm not asking you now that you think about Him or that you draw out a lot of concepts or make long and subtle reflections with your intellect. I'm not asking you to do anything more than look at Him" (W 26.3).[13] This kind of looking implies putting oneself in affective connection with the Other, in loving contemplation, without intellectual discourse.

In the second dwelling places she proposes looking at him and meditating on his passion: "Well, if we never look at him or reflect on what we owe Him and the death He suffered for us, I don't know how we'll be able to know Him or do works in His service; and what value can faith have without works and without joining them to the merits of

---

a sense of emptiness and abandonment (see L 22.4). At the doctrinal level, she argued with the theologians of her time, refusing to accept the meaning they attributed to the humanity of Jesus in contemplative prayer. For her, Jesus is the way and the mediation to go to the Father (see IC 6.7.6). It seemed to her a lack of humility to not accept the humanity of Jesus, given that it implies a fundamental failure to accept one's own humanity and the sufferings of this life (see L 22.6). She makes an appeal to the testimony of the saints (see L 22.7) and finally reaches the anthropological and psychological argument: "We are not angels but we have a body. To desire to be angels while we are on earth . . . is foolishness" (L 22.10). See Tomás Álvarez, ed., *Diccionario de Santa Teresa* (Burgos, Spain: Monte Carmelo, 2002), 382–84.

13. Something similar happens in the bonding relationship between mother and baby as they make contact by looking at each other.

Jesus Christ, our Good? Or who will awaken us to love this Lord?" (IC 2.1.11).

When we look at him this way, contemplating the love he has for us and with what a high price he surrendered himself for us,[14] we are filled with an immense gratitude and desire to unite ourselves to him, taking up each day's cross (see Lk 14:27). "Embrace the cross your Spouse has carried and understand that this must be your task" (IC 2.1.7). The gaze of Teresa is the empathetic look that captures his love, moving her to return it.

The third dwelling places deal more specifically with how we respond to that great love we have received: "What can we do for a God so generous that He died for us, created us, and gives us being?" (IC 3.1.8).[15] Teresa recalls the rich young man (IC 3.1.7) and the personal calling of the Lord to follow him: it is necessary to die to oneself, leaving everything behind. The ascetic way that Teresa proposes begins with the loving, empathetic relationship with Christ on the cross, which not only arouses the desire to leave everything and give oneself completely to him, but also provides strength to do it.[16]

---

14. Again, love is the beginning for a relationship with God. "Love begets love" (L 22.14).

15. This text reminds us of the meditation that St. Ignatius puts at the end of the first week of the Spiritual Exercises when the person has experienced God's love and responds with a love born from gratitude: "Imagining Christ our Lord present and placed on the Cross. . . . Likewise, looking at myself, what I have done for Christ, what I am doing for Christ, what I ought to do for Christ." Ignatius of Loyola, *The Spiritual Exercises of St. Ignatius of Loyola*, trans. Elder Mullan (New York: P. J. Kenedy & Sons, 1914), 39.

16. "Aren't these the ones who for a long while now have considered how the Lord suffered and how good suffering is, and who have desired it?" (IC 3.2.5).

Although in these initial dwelling places Christ stays more in the shadows, Teresa identifies him as the close model to follow. Through the body and the senses she finds a bond with Christ. By gazing at him, she is affectively involved, and this in turn moves the will: she looks at his humility in order to imitate it, contemplates his passion to follow it by way of the cross, and gazes at him dying for love of us, in order to die to herself.

In summary, in the beginning of the process of the Castle we see the feminine perspective: although in the first dwelling places the relationship with God is vertical and unequal, from the very beginning a bond of connection is established between God and his creatures; they are created in his image and likeness, and for that reason, God's mystery and greatness are present in them. There is a continuity and connection between the mystery of God and his presence in the soul. This experience of being image, likeness, and presence of his mystery must have helped Teresa to overcome the cultural preconceptions about women and affirm her own dignity as a daughter of God. Teresa believed that God communicated with his creatures, including women: "It is possible in this exile for so great a God to commune with such foul-smelling worms" (IC 1.1.3), in spite of the prevailing opinion that women were incapable of mental prayer. She proposes that despite the great contrast between God and us, there is no separation. Jesus is the human mediator, directing her humanity toward himself; she fixes her eyes on him, establishing a relationship with him as her friend and close model to imitate. As she continues to look steadfastly at Christ, she identifies with him, awakening compassion for his sufferings, stirring up the first movement toward a generous love, a "love beyond all reason" (see IC 3.2.7).

The Relationship That Transforms: Being in Love

The relationship with God proposed in the fourth dwelling places and part of the fifth is one that is born in the center of the soul and involves the whole person.

Incorporating the Whole Person

In the fourth dwelling places, which serve as transition from the third to the fifth, two different aspects of the experience of relationship with God are found together: the natural and the supernatural (see IC 4.3.14). The natural aspects of the relationship (what we acquire through our own meditation) correspond to the first three dwelling places, and the supernatural aspects (gifts of God) are given in the three last dwelling places. There is a link between the natural and supernatural in the fourth dwelling places, where both exist simultaneously. When the supernatural experiences begin and continue in those dwelling places, there is a shift from the previous dwelling places, in that the graces arise differently.

Explaining the difference between consolations and delights (*contentos* and *gustos* in Teresian language)[17] in prayer, Teresa analyzes the distinction between the natural and the supernatural. *Contentos* refer to the tenderness, peace, and pleasant satisfaction that come from meditation, with the person's effort. *Gustos* are experiences that can be similar; their origin, however, is from God, and they transform the person. In the degrees of prayer, Teresa calls this the prayer of quiet (see L 14 and 15).

---

17. 41 See Kavanaugh and Rodriguez, *Collected Works, Vol. 2*, p.481, n.1

The source of the *contentos* is "the natural,"[18] and this kind of prayer is primarily a mental activity: "These souls work almost continually with the intellect, engaging in discursive thought and meditation" (IC 4.1.6). Hence, the relationship too is mainly a rational one; typically, the person's affectivity is not involved.[19]

In contrast, the delights (*gustos*)[20] are born of God in the center of the soul[21] where "the source of the water" (IC 4.2.3-4) is found, that is, God himself;[22] it is in these depths of the soul that God's grace is at work. There are three important aspects to note:

First, the *gustos* involve the whole person. In comparison with what happens with the *contentos*, here the grace of God, "the supernatural," involves all of the natural; the body, the

---

18. Teresa uses the term "natural" to refer to all that deals with the body, including the senses and faculties, as well as temperament and illnesses. "The term 'consolations (*contentos*),' I think, can be given to those experiences we ourselves acquire through our own meditation and petitions to the Lords, those that proceed from our own nature—although God in the end does have a hand in them. . . . But the consolations arise from the virtuous work itself that we perform, and it seems that we have earned them through our own effort and are rightly consoled for having engaged in such deeds. . . . In sum, joyful consolations in prayer have their beginning in our own human nature and end in God" (IC 4.1.4).

19. *Contentos* deal with the prayer of recollection, which she speaks about in the first degree of prayer in the little treatise on prayer in *The Book of Her Life*, 11–13.

20. The *gustos* correspond to the prayer of quiet that she explains in the brief treatise on prayer in *The Book of Her Life*, 14–15.

21. So it is not a matter of the heart, even though it is the heart that is dilated and enlarged, "but from another part, still more interior, as from something deep. I think this must be the center of the soul, as I later came to understand" (IC 4.2.5).

22. "From its own source which is God" (IC 4.2.4).

senses, and the faculties all participate in the same activity, in such a way that the whole of the person lives the experience communicated by God. "For certainly, as anyone who may have experienced it will see, the whole exterior enjoys this spiritual delight and sweetness" (IC 4.2.4). This is a qualitative leap in the process: the senses, faculties, and the whole body enter the interior of the castle.[23] Until now the soul has heard the "calls of the Lord" by means of words of good people, in sermons or through reading good books (see IC 2.1.3). Now, however, on hearing the "whistle of the Shepherd," all her feminine being is involved—body, senses, and faculties. She is awakened to love with all her being and thus participates in the experience of God not just as a human being but also as a woman.

There is also an expansion of the soul that begins in the fourth dwelling places. "It seems that since that heavenly water begins to rise from this spring I'm mentioning that is deep within us, it swells and expands our whole interior being, producing ineffable blessings; nor does the soul even understand

---

23. "Let us suppose that these senses and faculties (for I have already mentioned that these powers are the people of this castle . . .) have gone outside and have walked for days and years with strangers—enemies of the well-being of the castle. Having seen their perdition they've already begun to approach the castle even though they may not manage to remain inside because the habit of doing so is difficult to acquire. But still they are not traitors, and they walk in the environs of the castle. Once the great King, who is in the center dwelling place of this castle, sees their good will, He desires in His wonderful mercy to bring them back to Him. Like a good shepherd, with a whistle so gentle that even they themselves almost fail to hear it, He makes them recognize His voice and stops them from going so far astray so that they will return to their dwelling place. And this shepherd's whistle has such power that they abandon the exterior things in which they were estranged from Him and enter the castle" (IC 4.3.2).

what is given to it there" (IC 4.2.6). God acts in the persons, enriching them with his gifts: "The soul is left with such wonderful blessings because God works within it without anyone disturbing Him, not even ourselves" (IC 5.1.5).

Another aspect is that in these graces the soul experiences the Lord in its center: "His Majesty desires that the soul enjoy Him in its own center" (IC 5.1.12), in the "very interior part of ourselves" (IC 4.2.4). But what does this center of the soul mean? The very, very interior? To clarify this term I am going to refer to studies already conducted on this subject by various specialists[24] and to those contained in the previously cited dictionary of St. Teresa.[25] It seems that this term "center of the soul" is not found in the usual language of mystical tradition; rather, it is considered a direct reflection of Teresa's experience or personal reflection. She began using it after speaking with John of the Cross, who used a similar term: "my soul in the deepest center."[26] For now, it is important to note that the center of the castle is the center of the soul (IC 1.1.3) and that in the center of the soul are God (IC 1.2.8) and the spirit of the soul (IC 7.2.10). The process that she lives throughout the castle is one of being transformed into Christ in order to be able to enter into the center where God and the soul's own spirit (made to the image and likeness of God) are found. We will resume this theme later when dealing with the structural changes in the spiritual marriage

---

24. Antonio Más Arrondo, *Teresa de Jesús en el Matrimonio Espiritual* (Ávila, Spain: Institución Gran Duque de Alba de la Excma. Diputación Provincial, 1993), 384–403.

25. See Álvarez, *Diccionario*, 140–42.

26. Lucinio Ruano, ed., *San Juan de la Cruz. Obras completas* (Madrid: Biblioteca de Autores cristianos, 1974), 744.

in the seventh dwelling places, when the soul is united with Christ in the center of the soul.

Images and Relationship with Christ

The relationship with Christ then comes from the same center of the soul. The images that appear in the fifth mansions are of a relationship of intimacy and friendship, such as "brought her into the inner wine cellar" (IC 5.2.12), or of the Last Supper (see IC 5.2.13), which symbolize well the type of relationship that is being engendered. To enter into the wine cellar and have supper with the Lord means to be in loving union with him: "I understand this union to be the wine cellar where the Lord wishes to place us when He desires and as He desires. . . . His Majesty must place us there and enter Himself into the center of our soul" (IC 5.1.12). These experiences of God touching the soul awaken a love so great that it "takes it out of itself,"[27] disposing it to share God's life, sorrows, interests, and even his passion, so that the soul feels that it already belongs to God: "Since that soul now surrenders itself into His hands and its great love makes it so surrendered that it neither knows nor wants anything more than what He wants with her (for God will never, in my judgment, grant this favor save to a soul that He takes for His own), He desires that, without its understanding how, it may go forth from this union impressed with His seal" (IC 5.2.12).

Love Has Taken Her Out of Herself

This great love and passion is born of the "love of God as its root" (IC 5.3.9) and has two fundamental effects, *transformation* and

---

27. "The one whom Your love, Lord, has drawn out of himself" (SS 1.12).

love of neighbor. This new kind of love allows the person to be identified with Christ and through love to be transformed into him, to live as he lived.[28] To explain it, Teresa uses the beautiful metaphor of the transformation of the silkworm. The worm of the first dwelling places has begun to weave its cocoon[29] and to construct its home in Christ[30] in order to be transformed into a beautiful butterfly in the fifth dwelling places, living the virtues and attitudes of the Lord. This process occurs only through the action of the Holy Spirit. The person in love with God has already surrendered, and there is "a strong will to do something for God" (IC 4.3.9). The transformation is accomplished through the connection and loving identification with Christ.

The second effect is love of neighbor and the passion for "saving many souls." For Teresa, the love of others is not altruism but a love rooted deeply in love of God. One who is identified with Christ, united to Him by love and feels His compassion for others, suffers: "Perhaps the sorrow proceeds from the deep pain it feels at seeing that God is offended and

---

28. "Because the authentic preparation for these favors . . . is the desire to suffer and imitate the Lord" (IC 4.2.9); "When, daughters, will we imitate this great God? Oh, let us not think we are doing anything by suffering injuries, but we should very eagerly endure everything, and let us love the one who offends us since this great God has not ceased to love us even though we have offended Him very much. Thus the Lord is right in wanting all to pardon the wrongs done to them" (IC 6.10.4).

29. "Therefore, courage, my daughters! Let's be quick to do this work and weave this little cocoon by getting rid of our self-love and self-will, our attachment to any earthly thing, and by performing deeds of penance, prayer, mortification, obedience, and of all the other things you know" (IC 5.2.6).

30. "Well, once this silkworm is grown . . . it begins to spin the silk and build the house wherein it will die. I would like to point out here that this house is Christ" (IC 5.2.4).

little esteemed in this world and that many souls are lost" (IC 5.2.10). An internal knowledge of Jesus creates empathy with his feelings: "What must have been the feeling of our Lord Jesus Christ? And what kind of life must He have suffered since all things were present to Him and He was always witnessing the serious offenses committed against His Father?" (IC 5.2.14). Now completely in love with God, Teresa wants to live united to him, surrendering her life to others for love, as he did.

We have seen the effects of the union that comes through "supernatural grace." Teresa explains, however, that there are two different types of union: the union that is given as a free gift from God, which is what has just been explained, and the active union, which is the basis for the union that is given. Without the active union, the supernatural graces are not given. This union consists in loving God and neighbor: "Here in our religious life the Lord asks of us only two things: love of His Majesty and love of our neighbor. These are what we must work for. By observing them with perfection, we do His will and so will be united with Him" (IC 5.3.7).

We can achieve this active union if we make the effort to procure it. And the two unions will always be marked by love of neighbor, whether it be through supernatural grace or through personal effort. It is the only sure sign (IC 5.3.8) of true union: "Works are what the Lord wants! He desires that if you see a sister who is sick to whom you can bring some relief, you have compassion on her and not worry about losing this devotion; and that if she is suffering pain, you also feel it, and that, if necessary, you fast so that she might eat—not so much for her sake as because you know it is your Lord's desire. This is true union with His will" (IC 5.3.11).

In the two types of union, being a woman awakens Teresa to profound empathy and a sense of solidarity, being conscious that loving God is loving neighbor and vice versa. In the concrete examples of loving service that we just read, Teresa exhorts her sisters to have compassion and feel the other's pain and that they "fast so that she might eat." In all of them we perceive a profound connection, closeness, loving care, and solidarity with the sisters. And this connectedness to others is always rooted in her connectedness to Christ; she adds that you should do it "because you know it is your Lord's desire."

Being in love with Christ and his mission has lit a fire in her heart, and it multiplies good deeds through contact: "It always brings profit to other souls . . . and they catch fire from its fire" (IC 5.3.1). The love of Christ is not understood without apostolic zeal; rather, they form a unity: passion for God and passion for humanity are two faces of the same coin.

The temptation found in these dwelling places also has two aspects. The first is seeking God only for the delights (*gustos*) one feels in prayer. In response to this Teresa invites the readers to unite themselves with the crucified one, like those "who walk by the path of love as they ought to walk, that is, only so as to serve their Christ crucified; not only do these persons refuse to seek spiritual delights (*gustos*) from Him or to desire them but they beseech Him not to give them these favors during their lifetime" (IC 4.2.9).[31] The other aspect of the temptation can occur in relationship with others: directing love toward something or someone other

---

31. A similar statement (IC 6.9.17) apparently refers to Teresa herself and probably St. John of the Cross. See IC 6.9.17n14.

than God.[32] Here Teresa refers to a "love" that is self-centered, an attachment separate from God. Freedom comes from growing in love without self-interest: "The initial thing necessary for such favors is to love God without self-interest" (IC 4.2.9). As Teresa knows, women may be especially prone to this temptation because of their tendency toward feeling connected, whether it be attachment to spiritual delights or affection for certain people. The two temptations are purified in these and in the following dwelling places in order to give the woman greater freedom in giving herself to God and to others. At the same time she becomes firm in a detachment that frees her from any tendency to center on herself.

In summary, from the feminine relational perspective we can note three aspects. First, beginning with the supernatural experiences of the fourth dwelling places, all of Teresa's being as a woman participates in the relationship: the body, senses, and faculties are all included in the supernatural experience. This implies that the way of feeling and living the experience will be marked by the reality that she is a woman, as we have already begun to see in these dwelling places; it will be seen more fully in the sixth. Teresa is walking a path toward integration and unity of self, as her body and senses participate in the experiences of God. This tendency toward unity within her own self is intrinsically connected to her being a woman.

Second, the relationship of intimacy and union with Christ disposes Teresa to share his life, sorrows, and interests for the salvation of souls. She shows connection and solidarity

---

32. "But if it is careless about placing its affection in something other than Him, it loses everything. And the loss is as great as the favors He was granting her, and cannot be exaggerated" (IC 5.4.4).

with Christ, extending her love for him to the sisters of her community, considering them as another self, sympathizing with them, and involving herself in such a way that she can feel their needs and pain. She loves her sisters with an attitude of motherly care that extends to interest for the salvation of all souls.

Third, Teresa's feminine tendency to try to continue the bond of union in the delights (*gustos*), as well as in the attachment of certain friendships, keeps on being purified. Union with God and God's love of others is strengthened in detachment, reinforcing her individuality and autonomy and giving as its fruit a love that is born of God.

Toward Mutuality:
Love That Creates Solidarity

Once the process of transformation in Christ is initiated, the relationship is opened to growth toward mutuality.[33] The last

---

33. I chose the term "mutuality" based on the scale elaborated by Jeffrey Urist to measure the maturity of the object relations in the autobiographical stories he cites, such as in the Rorschach test. See Jeffrey Urist, "The Rorschach Test and Assessment of Object Relations," *Journal of Personality Assessment* 41, no. 1 (1977): 3–9. The scales focus on the progressive development toward a perception of oneself as someone separate and autonomous and at the same time capable of involving oneself in a relationship of mutuality with another person, investing one's energy empathetically, independently of one's own necessities. In a later investigation, Urist expresses it this way: "The capacity for empathy, involving an intense realistic investment in the subjective world of another, while still maintaining the sense of mutual autonomy." Jeffrey Urist, "Validity of the Rorschach Mutuality of Autonomy Scale: A Replication Using Excerpted Responses," *Journal of Personality Assessment* 46, no. 5 (1982): 451. This author assumes as background the stages of object relations elaborated by Kernberg.

chapter of the fifth dwelling places links with the next two chapters by means of the allegory of spiritual matrimony.[34] It begins with the step she expresses as "*venir a vistas*"—coming to look at one another for the first time, as in the first meeting of a prearranged marriage—and continues to betrothal and matrimony. Encountering this symbolism from marriage, we can ask what Teresa's concept of matrimony was. We are going to refer to her principal writings in order to unravel this idea; from there we can understand the relationship that she proposes with Christ in the dwelling places.[35] In *The Way of Perfection* she uses this comparison to lead her Discalced Carmelite nuns into the way of prayer: "Here below before getting married a person will know the other party, who he is and what he possesses. . . . Why should they try to prevent us from thinking about who this man is, who His Father is, what country He is going to bring me to, what good things He promises to give me, what His status is, how I can make Him happy and in what ways I can please Him, and from studying how I can conform my way of life to His?" (W 22.7).[36]

In other writings, Teresa explains how the women of her time were subject to men, living in an unequal relationship.[37] Speaking of her nuns, she explains that sometimes "they do

34. Chapter 4 of the fifth dwelling places was written after an interruption of almost five months. For that reason, that part of the fifth dwelling places has more unity with the sixth and seventh mansions. Note what is said about the genesis of the book in chapter 4 of this book.

35. In *The Book of Her Life*, the word *Husband* appears four times, *wife* appears once, and *marriage* does not appear at all.

36. In *The Way of Perfection*, the word *Husband* appears twenty-one times; *wife*, three times; and marriage, once.

37. In *The Book of the Foundations*, the word *husband* appears sixteen times; *wife*, twelve times; and *marriage*, twelve times.

not recognize the great favor God has granted them in choosing them for Himself and freeing them from being subject to a man who is often the death of them and who could also be, God forbid, the death of their souls" (F 31.46).

Since, as we have already seen, this comparison with human marriage was common in the sociohistorical environment of her time, we want to see how Teresa proposes this spiritual experience. What is unique in her presentation of the relationship with Christ? Teresian Christology, based on the humanity of Christ, speaks of the "betrothal that God enters into with souls," emphasizing his "humbling himself" toward us: "For it doesn't seem to us possible for a soul to commune in such a way with God. . . . He has left a salutary remedy to souls that love Him with a fervent love because they understand and see that it is possible for God to humble Himself so much" (SS 1.5).[38]

In what must have been shocking contrast to the society of her time, when women lived to please their husbands, Teresa presented Christ disposed to serve us: "The Lord, without deception, truly acts in such a way with us. He is the one who submits, and He wants you to be the lady with authority to rule; He submits to your will" (W 26.4). In the sacrament of the Eucharist, his self-giving stands out, even to the point of making himself a slave: "May this move your hearts, my daughters, to love your Spouse, for there is no slave who would willingly say he is a slave, and yet it seems that Jesus is honored to be one" (W 33.4). Following the process of "humbling" by surrendering oneself in love, in the seventh dwelling

---

38. In this book of *Meditations on the Song of Songs*, the word *Husband* appears eighteen times, *wife* appears forty-one times, and *marriage* does not appear.

places, when the spiritual marriage is already realized, she proposes that true spirituality is to follow this way of making oneself a slave, as Christ did: "Do you know what it means to be truly spiritual? It means becoming the slaves of God. Marked with His brand, which is that of the cross, spiritual persons, because now they have given Him their liberty, can be sold by Him as slaves of everyone, as He was" (IC 7.4.8).[39] Christ has given himself to the utmost, drawing close to us, to humanity, in the incarnation, dying as a slave on the cross, and remaining with us in the Eucharist.

With these experiences of a love that leads Christ to humble himself for her sake, the relationship begins to change: "He gives us permission to think that He, this true Lover, my Spouse and my Good, needs us" (SS 4.11). In the first three dwelling places, Teresa recovered her dignity as a woman in the image of God. In the fourth and fifth she is overwhelmed by the humiliation of Christ and his drawing close to the littlest ones and to her as a woman, in order to elevate her and transform her into himself.

With the metaphor of the transformation of silkworm to butterfly, Teresa now introduces the theme of new life generated by union with Christ. Through metaphors such as the isolation and loss that she has to suffer for the worm to die, she begins to present the dynamic of death-life in Christ, his paschal mystery. Moved by the fire of love, the persons are stronger and know more clearly what and how they want to live; with a new horizon before their eyes, they have a new way of seeing life, a new knowledge of the Lord Jesus.[40]

---

39. In *The Interior Castle*, the word *Husband* appears twenty-five times; *wife*, twelve times; and *marriage* twelve times.

40. "So whoever is in Christ is a new creation" (2 Cor 5:17).

Their affections have been decentered from themselves, converting them toward love of God and neighbor. Now is the moment to initiate something new, and on the horizon we catch a glimpse of a change toward another type of relationship with Christ.[41]

The image that prevails in these last dwelling places revolves around the allegory of the spiritual marriage. Christ appears as the Bridegroom, the Betrothed, and the Spouse; and the soul as the bride, the betrothed, and the wife. The relationship has passed from being vertical and distant to being horizontal, close, intimate, mutual, marked by "feminine" characteristics in the soul and "masculine" ones in Christ. In this new form of relationship, the will and the desires of both play equal parts, and the process of transformation continues until arriving at union.

"Venir a Vistas"

In her allegory of spiritual union, Teresa follows the stages of the prenuptial rites of her age. The first step consists in the couple getting to know each other and exchanging first gifts: "Here below when two people are to be engaged,

---

41. The change of horizon or having a new vision of things creates a different dialectic that comes from conversion. To take a step of growth the person has to change posture, in this case leave "the old." Bernard Lonergan expresses it this way: "The presence or absence of intellectual, of moral, of religious conversion gives rise to dialectically opposed horizons. While complementary or genetic differences can be bridged, dialectical differences involve mutual repudiation. Each considers repudiation of its opposites the one and only intelligent, reasonable, and responsible stand and, when sufficient sophistication is attained, each seeks a philosophy or a method that will buttress what are considered appropriate views on the intelligent, the reasonable, the responsible." Bernard Lonergan, *Method in Theology* (Toronto: University of Toronto Press, 1971), 247.

there is discussion about whether they are alike, whether they love each other, and whether they might meet together so as to become more satisfied with each other" (IC 5.4.4). Teresa explicitly states that for both parties, freedom to make the commitment is necessary; she also speaks of the importance of spending time looking at each other so that they may be "satisfied" and fall in love. She further clarifies that this soul knows well the good that the marriage will bring, and so she is disposed to do the spouse's will in everything. In the same manner His Majesty is very happy with her and grants her this grace that they may meet together (see IC 5.4.4).

The relationship of mutuality is initiated with Christ in his risen humanity.[42] This creates the possibility of involving all her humanity as a woman and entering into a relationship with someone who, being God, grants her the favor of having a relationship on equal terms because he has lowered himself[43] to us.[44] He reveals his greatness to her and at the same time makes himself one like her, a life companion. Because of the mutuality in the relationship, the consent and the freedom of both are required in order to formalize a commitment; if they are both free and in agreement, the contract is entered into. Now the couple has the right and the obligation to get

---

42. The great majority of the visions of Christ in the mystical stage are of the humanity of the risen Christ, who bears the marks of his passion: "This most sacred humanity in its risen form was represented to me completely, as it is in paintings" (L 28.3; see also IC 6.9.3–4).

43. "You've already often heard that God espouses souls spiritually. Blessed be His mercy that wants so much to be humbled!" (IC 5.4.3).

44. We can see this new process of relating within the new creation in Christ, who is married with humanity. Christ made flesh, one with us, invites us to be born again in a new humanity in him (see Gen 2:23; Rom 5:12–6:11).

to know each other, "*venir a vistas*." They "come to see each other"[45], which Teresa describes this way:

> He desired her to know Him more and that they might meet together, as they say, and be united. We can say that union is like this, for it passes in a very short time. In it there no longer takes place the exchanging of gifts, but the soul sees secretly who this Spouse is that she is going to accept. Through the work of the senses and the faculties she couldn't in any way or in a thousand years understand what she understands here in the shortest time. But being who He is, the Spouse from that meeting alone leaves her more worthy for the joining of hands, as they say. The soul is left so much in love that it does for its part all it can to avoid disturbing this divine betrothal. (IC 5.4.4)

By this *vista*, or gazing, she comes to understand who her intended spouse is, after which she remains totally in love.[46] The experience changes her; it leaves her "more worthy" so

---

45. In this period in Spanish culture it was the custom for the couple to become engaged without even meeting each other, without seeing each other's face, because the bride-to-be wore a veil over her face. Getting to know each other was a rite that involved looking at each other, face to face; in her experience of God, however, Teresa deepened the sense of this gazing, yielding a new understanding of God and his love.

46. Here we seem to find ourselves before the grace of religious conversion, as Lonergan describes it: "Religious conversion is being grasped by ultimate concern. It is other-worldly falling in love. It is total and permanent self-surrender without conditions, qualifications, reservations. . . . It is interpreted differently in the context of different religious traditions. For Christians it is God's love flooding our hearts through the Holy Spirit given to us" (Lonergan, *Method in Theology*, 240–41). Teresa's surrender without conditions or reservations is shown in her fidelity expressed in the purification of the sixth dwelling places that already touches the foundation of her personality.

that they "come to give their hands" (IC 5.4.4). The encounter with God continues making her more like him, so that they share a closer intimacy in the relationship. In the texts before the citation above when Teresa speaks of the "hands" of God, she refers to surrendering into God's hands (IC 5.2.12); but beginning with the *vistas* it includes joining hands with the Lord—a traditional and pivotal part of the marriage ceremony: "The Spouse . . . leaves her more worthy for the joining of hands" (IC 5.4.4); "All their fear is that God might allow them out of His hand to offend Him" (IC 6.7.3). In other passages of *The Book of Her Life* that describe these dwelling places, she speaks of the experience of this meeting: "It is left full of amazement; one of these favors is enough to change a soul completely, free it from the love of things, and make it love Him who it sees makes it capable, without any effort of its own, of blessings so great, who communicates secrets to it and treats it with such friendship and love that one cannot describe this in writing" (L 27.9).

By means of gazing at each other, the lovers come to know each other; they "understand and show the love that they have."[47] "It's like the experience of two persons here on earth who love each other deeply and understand each other well; even without signs, just by a glance, it seems, they understand each other. This must be similar to what happens in the vision; without our knowing how, these two lovers gaze directly at each other, as the Bridegroom says to the Bride in the Song of Songs" (L 27.10).

---

47. "For God and the soul understand each other only through the desire His Majesty has that it understand Him, without the use of any other means devised to manifest the love these two friends have for each other" (L 27.10).

From gazing steadily, the soul has stayed wounded by love.[48] The image of the beloved has stayed impressed on this bride, and now she desires nothing more than to look at him again: "That meeting left such an impression that the soul's whole desire is to enjoy it again" (IC 6.1.1). The Lord, however, "still wants it to desire this more, and He wants the betrothal to take place at a cost; it is the greatest of blessings" (IC 6.1.1). So a process is begun that deepens and strengthens love as it is being tested.

A particularly feminine characteristic of her relationship with Christ is Teresa's desire to look at Christ, as a way of remaining connected to him. Teresa liked to contemplate images of the humanity of Christ. After her visions, especially beginning with the seventh dwelling places, she had several images of Christ painted; she was very devoted to these images.[49]

In summary, in the process leading to the spiritual marriage, the relationship is clearly marked by a feminine identification of the soul as bride, betrothed, and wife. In the first edition of *The Way of Perfection* (the "Códice Escorial") which censors made her correct, Teresa refers to the betrothal that takes place not only in the Carmelites, or in women, or

---

48. "Well then, let us, with the help of the Holy Spirit, speak of the sixth dwelling places, where the soul is now wounded with love for its Spouse" (IC 6.1.1).

49. Teresa had reproduced as paintings the imaginary visions of Christ, of the Trinity, and of the Virgin Mary. Christ tied to the column is very well documented. Those of Christ resurrected with the marks of the passion are those of the spiritual marriage, and there are two: one is in the monastery of Burgos, and the other is kept in the monastery of San José in Ávila. See Antonio Más Arrondo, *Acercar el cielo* (Cantabria, Spain: Sal Terrae, 2004), 256–61.

in other consecrated people, but in all the baptized: "We—and all souls—are betrothed by baptism" (CE 38,1).[50] She herself invites all those who read *The Interior Castle* to live this dimension of being the bride of Christ, bringing the feminine dimension of the church to life. Teresa narrates the personal account of her relationship with Christ from her experience of being a woman who is loved. This lived experience leaves her "more worthy" and causes her to break from the sociocultural concept of the marriage relationship that was held in her time. Christ, by the great love he shows her, restores her dignity and transforms her into himself. By this transformation she reproduces the image of Christ for the church community. She is the bride in her relationship with Christ and, at the same time, she is the image of Christ in relationship to the church.

"The Betrothal"

According to Teresa's outline of mystical development, the "betrothal" takes place in the sixth dwelling places, which are places of transition and preparation for the spiritual marriage. In these dwelling places the soul has to be purified: "It's natural that what is worth much costs much. Moreover, if the suffering is to purify this soul so that it might enter the seventh dwelling place . . . it is as small as a drop of water in the sea" (IC 6.11.6). This is necessary so that the soul can receive the gifts of the Lord: "In this pain the soul is purified and fashioned or purged like gold in the crucible

---

50. The first redaction of the *Way of Perfection*, known as the *Escorial*, is kept on display in the royal library of El Escorial in Spain. The quote here is translated from Enrique Llamas and others, eds, *Santa Teresa de Jesús Obras Completas*, 750, n.4

so that the enameled gifts might be placed there in a better way" (L 20.16).[51]

And what does this purification consist of? In the *vistas* the Bridegroom has left Teresa "wounded with love " (IC 6.1.1), and she is willing to go through anything for God, from whom comes her strength.[52] She is already in love with God, and loves her neighbor as well. The Lord, however, touches her to the depths of her personality, including her innate preferences and all that might limit her freedom to love and follow him. This purification affects all of her relationships.

Teresa's Relationship with God

In her relationship with God, Teresa is purified by strong experiences of both the presence and the absence of God. The experiences of God's presence continue transforming her, making her more like Christ, her betrothed, confirming her in love that is mutual, and making her love increase. She defines these experiences as "impulses so delicate and refined, for they proceed from very deep within the interior part of the soul" (IC 6.2.1), where God awakens the soul for love (see IC

---

51. The complete passage in *The Book of Her Life* corresponding to the sixth dwelling places is as follows: "The Lord told me not to fear and to esteem this gift more than all the others He had granted me. In this pain the soul is purified and fashioned or purged like gold in the crucible so that the enameled gifts might be placed there in a better way, and in this prayer it is purged of what otherwise it would have to be purged of in purgatory" (L 20.16; see also L 30.14).

52. "There, the soul fears nothing and is absolutely determined to overcome every obstacle for God. And the reason is that it is always so closely joined to His Majesty that from this union comes its fortitude" (IC 6.1.2).

6.2.2, IC 6.2.8), with ecstasies,[53] delicious sorrows,[54] flight of the spirit,[55] delightful enkindling,[56] conversations with God,[57] experiences of jubilation and rejoicing,[58] intellectual visions,[59]

---

53. "His Majesty from the interior of the soul makes the spark we mentioned increase, for He is moved with compassion in seeing the soul suffer so long a time from its desire. All burnt up, the soul is renewed like the phoenix, and one can devoutly believe that its sins are pardoned. Now that it is so pure, the Lord joins it with Himself, without anyone understanding what is happening except these two" (IC 6.4.3). "The soul, while it is made one with God, is placed in this room of the empyreal heaven that we must have interiorly. For clearly, the soul has some of these dwelling places since God abides within it. And although the Lord must not want the soul to see these secrets every time it is in this ecstasy, for it can be so absorbed in enjoying Him that a sublime good like that is sufficient for it, sometimes He is pleased that the absorption decrease and the soul see at once what is in that room" (IC 6.4.8).

54. "The pain is great, although delightful and sweet" because "He is present, but He doesn't want to reveal the manner in which He allows Himself to be enjoyed" (IC 6.2.2).

55. "God wishes that the soul . . . should understand that in itself it no longer has any part to play; and it is carried off with a noticeably more impetuous movement" (IC 6.5.2); "A huge wave rises up so forcefully that it lifts high this little bark that is our soul" (IC 6.5.3).

56. "A delightful enkindling will come upon it as though a fragrance were suddenly to become so powerful as to spread through all the senses . . . only for the sake of making one feel the Spouse's presence there. The soul is moved with a delightful desire to enjoy Him" (IC 6.2.8).

57. "For the very spirit that speaks puts a stop to all other thoughts and makes the soul attend to what is said" (IC 6.3.18).

58. "It is, in my opinion, a deep union of the faculties; but our Lord nonetheless leaves them free that they might enjoy this joy—and the same goes for the senses—without understanding what it is they are enjoying or how they are enjoying . . . for the joy is so excessive the soul wouldn't want to enjoy it alone but wants to tell everyone about it so that they might help this soul praise our Lord" (IC 6.6.10).

59. "The further a soul advances, the more it is accompanied by the good Jesus" (IC 6.8.1). "It will happen while the soul is heedless of any thought about such a favor being granted to it, and though it never had a thought

and imaginary visions.[60] These signs of the love of God cause her to "go out of herself" and dissolve in loving service; she feels disposed to live either in the desert or in the middle of the world in order "to play a part in getting even one soul to praise God more" (IC 6.6.3).

Referring to this possibility of preaching and announcing the kingdom, a complaint similar to one in her first redaction of *The Way of Perfection*[61] appears in these dwelling places: Teresa feels an apostolic fire burning within her, urging her to announce the kingdom, to participate in the public mission of the church in order to collaborate in the "salvation of souls." But the culture of her time did not permit a woman to play this role publicly, and she grieved: "A woman in this stage of prayer is distressed by the natural hindrance there is to her entering the world, and she has great envy of those who have

---

that it deserved this vision, that it will feel Jesus Christ, our Lord, beside it. Yet it does not see Him, either with the eyes of the body or with those of the soul. This is called an intellectual vision; I don't know why. . . . However, she [the person who received this favor, Teresa herself] knew so certainly that it was Jesus Christ, our Lord, who showed Himself to her in that way" (IC 6.8.2). "For this latter [this presence] brings great interior benefits and effects that couldn't be present if the experience were caused by melancholy; nor would the devil produce so much good; nor would the soul go about with such peace and continual desires to please God, and with so much contempt for everything that does not bring it to Him" (IC 6.8.3).

60. "He shows it clearly His most sacred Humanity in the way He desires; either as He was when He went about in the world or as He is after His resurrection. And even though the vision happens so quickly that we could compare it to a streak of lightning, this most glorious image remains so engraved on the imagination that I think it would be impossible to erase it until it is seen by the soul in that place where it will be enjoyed without end" (IC 6.9.3). She says that the imaginary visions are surely more advantageous because they are more conformed to our nature inasmuch as they are images (see IC 6.9.1).

61. See C.E. bracketed insert in W 3.7 and 3.7n2.

the freedom to cry out and spread the news abroad about who this great God of hosts is" (IC 6.6.3). She feels tied up with bonds that keep her from flying to where she wants to go (see IC 6.6.4), and she makes a petition in which she presents herself as the weaker part of humanity,[62] asking the Lord to act through her, so that it will be obvious that grace comes from God and not from her. She prays: "Let your grandeur appear in a creature so feminine and lowly, whatever the cost to her, so that the world may know that this grandeur is not hers at all and may praise You. This praise is what she desires, and she would give a thousand lives— if she had that many—if one soul were to praise You a little more through her" (IC 6.6.4). The soul that has experienced the love of God so strongly cannot do anything except use its life totally in his service and strive to overcome whatever kind of barrier that might hinder it.

Each time she experiences the presence of God, it ignites more apostolic zeal in her. But what happens when the experiences have passed? She finds herself in exile and solitude, feeling deprived of God's presence:

> The reasoning faculty is in such a condition that the soul is not the master of it, nor can the soul think of anything else than of why it is grieving, of how it is absent from its Good, and of why it should want to live. It feels a strange solitude because no creature in all the earth provides it company, nor do I believe would any heavenly creature, not being the One whom it loves; rather, everything torments it. But the soul sees that it is like a person hanging, who cannot

---

62. As Jesus himself did, making himself weak and small, in order to reach the ends of the earth.

support himself on any earthly thing; nor can it ascend to heaven. On fire with this thirst, it cannot get to the water; and the thirst is not one that is endurable but already at such a point that nothing will take it away. Nor does the soul desire that the thirst be taken away save by that water of which our Lord spoke to the Samaritan woman. Yet no one gives such water to the soul. (IC 6.11.5)

This privation is already a purification, inviting her to accept solitude and exile and "to wait for the mercy of God" (IC 6.1.10).

In the sixth dwelling places, Teresa narrates experiences of strong union with God and also episodes of absence and separation, together with the purifications that they involved for her. For Teresa these constituted her dark night—a night that did not lead to despair, however, but one that made total abandonment to the mercy of God possible. On beginning the seventh dwelling places, she explains why this separation was still possible in the betrothal, since the full marriage had not yet taken place: "The spiritual betrothal is different [from marriage], for the two often separate. And the union is also different because, even though it is the joining of two things into one, in the end the two can be separated and each remains by itself. We observe this ordinarily, for the favor of union with the Lord passes quickly, and afterward the soul remains without that company; I mean, without awareness of it" (IC 7.2.4).[63]

---

63. This passage also speaks of what the betrothal is: "Let us say that the union is like the joining of two wax candles to such an extent that the flame coming from them is but one, or that the wick, the flame, and the wax are all one. But afterward one candle can be easily separated from the other and there are two candles; the same holds for the wick" (IC 7.2.4).

Teresa's Relationship to Herself

In Teresa's relationship to herself we can see aspects of both body and mind. In these dwelling places her body participates more intensely: feeling, suffering, and enjoying as a woman.[64] "The Lord is wont also to send it the severest illnesses" (IC 6.1.6); when the soul arrives at this stage, the pains can be so intense that it prefers any martyrdom so that the pains pass more quickly. In Teresa's case, however, this infirmity continued throughout her life (she spent more than forty years with illnesses; see IC 6.1.7), making her aware of her body and its limits. So she proposes living this aspect of suffering by "enduring" with Christ; by means of her body she is united to his humanity. The purification was already begun in the first dwelling places, where the reader was invited to freedom from excessive care of one's body and health, in order to direct the body totally to the service of the Lord.[65] In these mansions, she is now disposed to share the pains of the passion and receive graces in which the body will participate: "Do you think that it is a small disturbance for a person to be very much in his senses and see his soul carried off (and in the case of some, we have read, even the body with the soul) without knowing where that soul is going, what or who does this, or

---

64. Of the fifty-one times that the word *body* appears in the dwelling places, it is found twenty-one times (41 percent) in the sixth mansions, without counting synonyms such as natural, senses, temperament, or the illnesses that enter the body and on occasion the imagination that enters within the natural.

65. She had already said this in the third mansions: "Let the prelates [superiors] take care of our bodily needs; that's their business. As for ourselves, we should care only about moving quickly so as to see this Lord. . . . We could be deceived by worry about our health" (IC 3.2.8).

how? At the beginning of this swift movement there is not so much certitude that the rapture is from God" (IC 6.5.1).

Through the senses the body also participates in rejoicing in God's presence. "It is, in my opinion, a deep union of the faculties; but our Lord nonetheless leaves them free that they might enjoy this joy—and the same goes for the senses—without understanding what it is they are enjoying or how they are enjoying it" (IC 6.6.10). The same body, in the measure to which it is being reoriented to the Lord, feels the effects of his friendship and closeness. Teresa noted it in one of her communications with her confessors: "I have experienced for more than a half year that at least when I am receiving Communion I noticeably and clearly feel bodily health" (ST 1.23).

In the experience of the absence of God, Teresa also speaks of psychological effects. She notes the "weaknesses" that women may experience because of a remnant of selfishness that stays in the human being and needs to be purified. In solitude, she has remained very vulnerable and sensitive to the least sign of the presence of God, which she calls "news" (words, memories, images, and songs).[66] On hearing or remembering the love of God, she "went out of herself" with the subsequent bodily repercussions: she was unable to speak, her extremities grew very cold, and she seemed to be in a kind of suspended animation, as observers could not detect her breathing (see IC 6.4.13). The soul, so much in need of God's presence, involved all of her "natural being" in its desire, and she sought this total absorption of the whole body in the experience of God.

---

66. Listening to a sister sing the song "May My Eyes See You" after some days of dryness and absence, Teresa was taken up in ecstasy, as she relates in several places (Ltr 30 to Isabel de Jesús Jimena at the end of 1570; SS 7.2).

Such overwhelming desire can sometimes provoke what Teresa calls "natural weakness." "It can happen in persons with a weak constitution, as is so with women, that any spiritual force will overcome the natural powers, and the soul will be absorbed" (IC 6.4.9). The soul can fall into the desire to "remain always in that state of delight" (IC 6.7.13). She confesses that this once happened to her, when she put aside the humanity of Jesus Christ because she had been advised to avoid the corporal; she tried to remain "indulging myself in that absorption, waiting for that gift" (IC 6.7.15). Teresa urges her sisters to "strive to free yourself from this error and avoid such absorption with all your strength" (IC 6.7.13). She advises looking at the works of Christ: "Let them believe me and not be so absorbed, as I have said elsewhere. Life is long, and there are in it many trials, and we need to look at Christ our model, how He suffered them, and also at His apostles and saints" (IC 6.7.13).

Teresa also warns that women sometimes have the weakness of "false tears" (IC 6.6.8) and informs us that when tears are not "peaceful," the result is "that these persons become so weak that they will afterward be unable either to pray or to keep their rule" (IC 6.6.7). She advises: "Let's not think that everything is accomplished through much weeping, but set our hands to the task of hard work and virtue" (IC 6.6.9). Attributing tears more to women than to men is not only a cultural norm of expecting women to show their feelings (which is considered a weakness) but is also due to the fact that women are usually more in touch with their own feelings and express them more strongly than men do.

In her "experience of solitude and exile," Teresa asks for the grace to be able to accept separation and detachment from

God's presence, so that, from the feminine perspective, these experiences also present another occasion of purification. The best solution for enduring these moments of darkness is for the soul to abandon itself to God's mercy and do works of charity: "They [times of darkness] are indescribable, for they are spiritual afflictions and sufferings that one cannot name. The best remedy (I don't mean for getting rid of them, because I don't find any, but so that they may be endured) is to engage in external works of charity and to hope in the mercy of God who never fails those who hope in Him" (IC 6.1.13).

The purification of these "feminine weaknesses" certainly involves the "way of feeling" and the tendency to try to remain in connection. Actually persons of both genders can deeply desire to be in union with the Beloved, as one who is held, contained, or possessed, although men and women may have different ways of expressing it. Men, for example, may tend more toward using power or achievement as a means of controlling relationships with others, while women may tend more to foster relationships with others, to maintain the connectedness. Such tendencies, whatever they may be, carry through to the relationship with the Beloved: a man might try to possess God through fulfilling the law or by achieving good, and a woman might try to maintain an emotional connection. In both men and women there needs to be a purification of their own selfishness: the male tends to disconnection and isolation; and the woman, to connection and empathy.[67] In order to become gifts for the Other and for others, they must both be liberated from their own egoistic tendencies.

---

67. See Nancy Chodorow, "Gender, Relation and Difference in Psychoanalytic Perspective," in *Feminism and Psychoanalytic Theory*, 99–113 (New Haven, Conn.: Yale University Press, 1989).

Thus, we can say that gender necessarily affects everyone's way of living mystical experiences. In the case of Teresa, as woman, the great love she lives tends to promote "the natural" in order to feel and become involved, whether by tears or by absorption. For everyone, liberation consists in letting go of egoistical pleasures and being fully present to the reality of life, looking at Christ and practicing virtues.

Teresa's Relationship with Others

In her relationship with others, the purification is found in several forms. It may be with *external distress*, from what Teresa calls *outcries*, from her nuns as well as from confessors and friends (see IC 6.1.3). It consists of criticism, grumbling, accusations, "a thousand kinds of ridicule" (IC 6.1.3). And this continues her whole life long. Freedom comes when she leaves aside "honor," what we would call today her self-image. When she discovers that she receives good from this contempt and criticism, it awakens love of her enemies: "And when the soul reaches the stage at which it pays little attention to praise, it pays much less to disapproval; on the contrary, it rejoices in this and finds it a very sweet music. . . . Blame does not intimidate the soul but strengthens it. Experience has already taught it the wonderful gain that comes through this path. . . . It acquires a special and very tender love for its persecutors. It seems to it that they are greater friends and more advantageous than those who speak well of it" (IC 6.1.5).

The purification may be accompanied by internal pains, *dryness* (IC 6.1.8), and *depression* (IC 6.1.13). The incomprehension and lack of confidence of her confessors also increased her insecurity and fear of being deceived, provoking in her an anxiety that was almost unbearable (IC 6.1.8). The result was that her bad mood and gloomy aspect were very obvious to others (see IC 6.1.13), and the only thing that helped her was to abandon herself to the mercy of God.

Purification may also come through *experiences of God* that touch the most profound roots of her personality and change her relationships from within. We will refer in a particular way to the imaginary vision of the humanity of Christ (IC 6.9.2–5). This experience is found in *The Interior Castle* (IC 6.9.3–4) and is described in greater detail in *The Book of Her Life*, with the implications that it had for her personally:

> The vision of Christ left upon me an impression of His most extraordinary beauty, and the impression remains today; one time is sufficient to make this imprint. How much deeper it becomes as the Lord grants this favor more often! The benefit I received was most advantageous, and this is what it consisted of: I had a serious fault that did me much harm; it was that when I began to know that certain persons like me, and I found them attractive, I became so attached that my memory was bound strongly by the thought of them. There was no intention to offend God, but I was happy to see these persons and think about them and about the good things I saw in them. This was something so harmful it was leading my soul seriously astray. After I beheld the extraordinary beauty of the Lord, I didn't see anyone who in comparison with Him seemed to attract me or occupy my thoughts. By turning my gaze just a little inward to behold the image I have in my soul, I obtained such freedom in this respect that everything I see here below seems loathsome when compared to the excelling and beautiful qualities I beheld in this Lord. (L 37.4)

The encounter with the humanity of Christ has involved all of her psychodynamic sexual affectivity in an intense and total way. This encounter has been so much more powerful than all the experiences of God of the past that in addition to leaving her unable to ever forget it, it has profoundly changed her (see IC 6.4.5). Her affect and emotions, and her way of loving and reacting are purified, reaching to the deepest levels of her personality,[68] in order to make her more

68. Teresa of Jesus has been the subject of innumerable psychological studies. Tomás Álvarez, one of the foremost specialists in St. Teresa, has given us a summary and analysis of these studies from the perspective of spiritual theology, in *Santa Teresa a contraluz* (Burgos, Spain: Monte Carmelo, 2004). From the beginning, it seems that two important aspects that interest us converge in this theme: her personality and the external manifestations of the mystical experiences. In recent years, the study of mysticism and psychology has sparked tremendous interest, and Teresa serves as an ideal subject for it because we have her own narration. At present we can see a greater dialogue between psychology and mystical experiences, although this dialogue doesn't always succeed in establishing the necessary foundations in order to converge in a single adequate interdisciplinary perspective. It is increasingly understood, however, that the saints each had a unique personality style with concrete characteristics that reveal aspects of the unconscious. Here are cited only a few studies among the many: Antoine Vergote, "Una mirada psicológica sobre la mística de Teresa de Ávila," in *Actas del Congreso Internacional Teresiano*, ed. Teófanes Egido Martinez, 883–96, vol. 2 (Salamanca, Spain: Salamanca University, 1982); Mercedes Navarro Puerto, *Psicología y Mística. Las Moradas de Santa Teresa* (Madrid: Ed. San Pio X, 1992); Terrance G. Walsh, "Writing Anxiety in Teresa's Interior Castle," *Theological Studies* 56 (1995): 251–75; Frohlich, *Intersubjectivity of the Mystic*; Carole Slade, *St. Teresa of Ávila: Author of a Heroic Life* (Berkeley: University of California Press, 1995); Alison Weber, *Teresa of Ávila and the Rhetoric of Femininity* (Princeton, N.J.: Princeton University Press, 1990); Jill Matus, "Saint Teresa, Hysteria, and Middlemarch," *Journal of the History of Sexuality* 1, no. 2 (1990): 215–40; Elena Carrera, *Teresa of Ávila's Autobiography: Authority, Power and the Self in Mid-Sixteenth-Century Spain* (London: Legenda, 2005); and others. We are far from the times in which psychology and mysticism appeared as irreconcilable

like Christ. With great intelligence and creativity, Teresa lived an intense affective life from childhood and adolescence, attached to her father and brothers, with an overflowing imagination and youthful challenges in navigating her own sexuality and affective attachments.[69] And although it is difficult to evaluate a personality from a time and culture so different from our own, we recognize today that there are

points of view. If, as has been said, there were manifestations of hysterical personality in Teresa, it was thought that they would annul the truth of all the experiences she had lived. There was no true distinction, either in the field of spiritual theology or in the field of psychology, since in the background the conflict between psychology and spiritual theology was played out between anthropological views that were at times irreconcilable. Many studies, made without sufficiently deep knowledge of Teresa, considered some isolated manifestations outside the general context of her life, with the result that they confused an ecstasy with an epileptic attack. See Esteban García-Albea, *Teresa de Jesús, una ilustre epiléptica* (Madrid: Huerga y Fierro Editores, 1995). Analyzing from different and reductive viewpoints, without any dialogue with the experience that the person lived, it is difficult to arrive at any measure of objectivity. We now find ourselves in a time in which it is possible to establish a more flexible and open dialogue between psychology and mysticism. Teresa exerted great effort in introspection in order to discern the possible deceptions of her mystical experiences, and in the text we can perceive her enormous capacity for analyzing and scrutinizing herself. She knows how to differentiate between an experience arising from weakness or melancholy and one in which there is true revelation and knowledge of God. One must consider that normally the action of grace is given in subjects with a specific personality and that the senses, faculties, and the body participate. God reveals himself and manifests himself within our own unique way of being. Teresa provides criteria for discerning whether the experiences are from God or not, paying special attention to behavior and posing implicit questions: Does the person who has these experiences carry out works of God, that is, Gospel works? Is the person able to face reality and transform it?

69. See *The Book of Her Life*, chapters 7 and 8. "I began to go from pastime to pastime, from vanity to vanity, from one occasion to another" (L 7.1).

aspects of her life that indicate characteristics of a histrionic personality touched by the grace of God.[70]

By experiencing the humanity of Christ, Teresa was liberated from the tendency (rooted in the culture and in her own personality) to admire men and depend on them emotionally, enslaving the richest aspect of her being woman: relationships. On the other hand, the cultural inheritance that made women (who were "unlettered" or at least not formally educated) have to go to men (who were lettered) to learn the truth from them was somewhat undermined by the doubts and the great sufferings that her confessors caused her. Eventually, the inability to find the truth in these learned confessors made her realize that only in God is supreme truth: "God will show within Himself a truth that seems to leave in obscurity all those there are in creatures, and one understands very clearly that God alone is Truth, unable to lie" (IC 6.10.5). Teresa's relationship with God was liberating her from the limits of her own personality; she was being freed from the mental constructs that

---

70. With respect to this point, Vergote tells us, "I scarcely dare to use the technical word because unfortunately it has a connotation of disdain, but Teresa of Ávila had a psychic structure markedly hysterical. Not that she was neurotic, although she could have become so if it were not for the extraordinary work on herself, a work of purification and growth in her unconscious. . . . This does not explain the fact that she had oriented towards God the powerful desire of attachment, love and pleasure, because it was the message of faith that proposed this objective. So there is in her both a desire that has its origin in the unconscious together with a desire that awakens, that even causes, the religious message. In this message she understood the promise that in God she would find the union of love she desired so much. This conjunction of psychological dynamics and the promise of the religious message helps us to understand the particular mystic trajectory of Teresa, with all her strange phenomena and the difficulties that she finds in this trajectory." Vergote, "Una Mirada psicológica," 892.

the culture had been imposing with regard to what a woman should be and the role that she ought to play.

In summary, in this phase of preparation for the spiritual marriage, various aspects of the female perspective entered into play. Her very feminine way of relating and of living experiences with clear tendencies to connection is purified from selfishness and personal pleasure by means of separation, solitude, and the experience of exile and misunderstanding. Yet the profound relationship she had with God and the desire to "save souls" made Teresa both question and free herself from those cultural traditions that she had absorbed concerning the role of women. In keeping with her sixteenth-century environment, she questioned the possibility of public ministry for women in the church. At that same time, she was liberated from the culturally imposed affective dependence on and idealization of men, which had been strengthened by the tendencies of her personality. In Teresa's time, men were the apparent bearers of power, and only men accomplished heroic works, while women were regarded as merely utilitarian and subservient to men. Teresa was also freed from a cultural dependency that was imposed by the same society, awarding privilege to men as possessors of the truth because of their education. She discovered that truth is to be found only in God, thus achieving an astounding liberty in her relationships with those who were educated. Teresa's uniquely feminine and personalized affective sense engaged the whole person in the relational process. Her experiences of God were thus distinctly feminine and showed the body's role as she journeyed through the dwelling places.

Spiritual Marriage: Life-Giving Love of Humanity

We are now in the last stage of the castle, where Teresa's relationships have reached maturity. Here we discover how real love is reflected in the faces of actual people and at the same time is open to a universal love for all humanity. In this phase Teresa lived in total self-giving to the service of the church and of humanity, trying to build a world in which it is possible to love God and neighbor.

Intimacy with Christ, Openness to a Third

First, we note that in these dwelling places Teresa is describing a marriage relationship, which she considers to be the greatest intimacy and commitment that can exist between two persons. In Teresa's view, in a relationship of this depth, intimacy and love grow in proportion to openness to and love of others. This process was begun in the first dwelling places, and in the seventh it is made explicit: the closer we are to God, the more we love our neighbor. Thus we have a relationship that is strengthened and grows until it becomes mutual belonging, in which commitment and intimacy are the keys to openness to others. The relationship is always progressively opened more and more to the presence of a third: to others nearby, to her sisters in community (see IC 5.3.11), to the church (see IC 4.3.10, IC Epil 4), and, in its fullness, to all humankind. (IC 7.3.6). This love is open and fertile, generating new life.

Teresa indicates that the objective of receiving these graces is to be transformed in Christ and to be united to his suffering in order to participate in his redemptive mission for humanity:

> It will be good, sisters, to tell you the reason the Lord grants so many favors in this world. . . . I want to tell you again here lest someone think that the reason is solely for the sake of giving delight to these souls; that thought would be a serious error. His Majesty couldn't grant us a greater favor than to give us a life that would be an imitation of the life His beloved Son lived. Thus I hold for certain that these favors are meant to fortify our weakness, as I have said here at times, that we may be able to imitate Him in His great sufferings. (IC 7.4.4)

Thus the grace that one receives in the spiritual marriage is similar to that which made the Word become flesh and espouse humankind: to surrender his life for the salvation of the world. "His food is that in every way possible we draw souls that they may be saved and praise him always" (IC 7.4.12).

The center of this process is the humanity of Christ as bridge and union between the human and the divine. In the seventh dwelling places we find the spiritual marriage described by means of an imaginary vision of the humanity of Christ.[71] We have a detailed description of this grace, in the "accounts of conscience" given to her confessors:

---

71. "The first time the favor is granted, His Majesty desires to show Himself to the soul through an imaginative vision of His most sacred humanity so that the soul will understand and not be ignorant of receiving this sovereign gift. With other persons the favor will be received in another form. With regard to the one of whom we are speaking, the Lord represented Himself to her, just after she had received Communion, in the form of shining splendor, beauty, and majesty, as He was after His resurrection, and told her that now it was time that she consider as her own what belonged to Him and that He would take care of what was hers, and He spoke other words destined more to be heard than to be mentioned" (IC 7.2.1).

While at the Incarnation in the second year that I was prioress, on the octave of the feast of St. Martin, when I was receiving Communion, Father John of the Cross who was giving me the Blessed Sacrament broke the host to provide for another sister. I thought there was no lack of hosts but that he wanted to mortify me because I had told him it pleased me very much when the hosts were large (not that I didn't understand that the size made no difference with regard to the Lord's being wholly present, even when the particle is very small). His Majesty said to me: "Don't fear, daughter, for no one will be a party to separating you from Me," making me thereby understand that what just happened didn't matter. Then He appeared to me in an imaginative vision, as at other times, very interiorly, and He gave me His right hand and said: "Behold this nail; it is a sign you will be My bride from today on. Until now you have not merited this; from now on not only will you look after My honor as being the honor as your Creator, King, and God, but you will look after it as My true bride. My honor is yours, and yours Mine." This favor produced such an effect in me I couldn't contain myself, and I remained as though entranced. I asked the Lord either to raise me from my lowliness or not grant me such a favor; for it didn't seem to me my nature could bear it. Throughout the whole day I remained thus very absorbed. Afterward I felt great pain, and greater confusion and affliction at seeing I don't render any service in exchange for such amazing favors. (ST 31; written November 1572; Teresa was then fifty-seven)

The text shows explicitly that a change is taking place in the relationship. She goes from being servant of her King and

Creator to a relationship of friendship with Christ, a relationship between equals, *tú a tú* (using the Spanish pronoun for a relationship of equals, as friends), "as a spouse." Christ and Teresa make a mutual commitment to each other: each loves the other, each is concerned wholly with the interests of the other. This change in the relationship takes her completely by surprise. Her "natural being" could not tolerate the experience, because she is so overwhelmed by her awareness of the greatness of God and the smallness of her being in the face of this great gift.

By means of this bond they belong to each other, totally and forever. Now they cannot be separated: "For He has desired to be so joined with the creature that, just as those who are married cannot be separated, He doesn't want to be separated from the soul" (IC 7.2.3). Another characteristic of the bond is that the union is forever: "The union is like what we have when rain falls from the sky into a river or fount; all is water, for the rain that fell from heaven cannot be divided or separated from the water of the river. Or it is like what we have when a little stream enters the sea, there is no means of separating the two. Or, like the bright light entering a room through two different windows; although the streams of light are separate when entering the room, they become one" (IC 7.2.4).

How is this experience of union different from others? What has happened in the soul so that they can never again be separated? Teresa says the difference is that here the union is in *the center of the soul*: "This secret union takes place in the very interior center of the soul, which must be where God Himself is, and in my opinion there is no need of any door for Him to enter . . . because everything that has been said up until now seems to take place by means of the senses and faculties, and this appearance of the humanity of the Lord must also. But that which comes to pass in the union of the spiritual marriage is very different. The Lord appears in this center of the soul" (IC 7.2.3).

It is at the center of the soul where the image of God is imprinted, where God dwells. There, in this center, is where the soul experiences union: "The soul, I mean the spirit, is made one with God" (IC 7.2.3), and "the soul always remains with its God in that center" (IC 7.2.4). (This aspect will be developed further in chapter 7.)

Love of Total Self-Giving

Through this union, the person continues being transformed, and Teresa shares with us some of its effects. We recall that in the sixth dwelling places the butterfly (the soul) found no place to alight and therefore "went about so anxious, everything frightened it and made it fly" (IC 7.3.12). Here, after the union in the depths of the soul, "the butterfly we mentioned dies, and with the greatest joy because her life is now Christ" (IC 7.2.5). It dies because now "it doesn't feel that solitude it did before since it enjoys such company" (IC 7.3.12). With this profound experience of God, what she called "weakness of nature" has disappeared: "When the soul arrives here all raptures are taken away. Only once in a while are they experienced and then without those transports and that flight of the spirit. They happen very rarely and almost never in public as they very often did before. Nor do the great occasions of devotion cause the soul concern as previously" (IC 7.3.12). The experience of divine and human union has settled Teresa's body, her natural being, and her

desires; now she lives serenely in the certitude of his continuous presence in the soul.

Other effects of the transforming relationship of love are
self-forgetfulness,[72] apostolic zeal,[73] the desire to suffer,[74] interior joy when persecuted,[75] a great desire not to die in order
to serve,[76] and a great detachment from everything,[77] which
occurs without dryness or agitation.[78] The person is fully

---

72. "This soul doesn't know or recall that there will be heaven or life
of honor for it, because it employs all it has in procuring the honor of
God. . . . Thus, the soul doesn't worry about all that can happen. It experiences strange forgetfulness, for, as I say, seemingly the soul no longer is
or would want to be anything in anything, except when it understands that
there can come from itself something by which the glory and honor of God
may increase even one degree" (IC 7.3.2).

73. "For no earthly thing would it fail to do all it can and understands
to be for the service of our Lord" (IC 7.3.3).

74. "The soul has a great desire to suffer, but not the kind of desire
that disturbs it as previously. . . . These souls . . . think everything His
Majesty does is good. If He desires the soul to suffer, well and good; if not it
doesn't kill itself as it used to" (IC 7.3.4).

75. "These souls also have a deep interior joy when they are persecuted,
with much more peace . . . and without any hostile feelings toward those
who do, or desire to do, them evil" (IC 7.3.5).

76. "They have just as great a desire to serve Him and that through
them He be praised and that they may benefit some soul if they can. For not
only do they not desire to die but they desire to live very many years suffering
the greatest trials if through these they can help that the Lord be praised,
even though in something very small. . . . Their glory lies in being able
some way to help the Crucified" (IC 7.3.6).

77. "There is a great detachment from everything and a desire to be
always either alone or occupied in something that will benefit some soul" (IC
7.3.8).

78. "There are almost never any experiences of dryness or interior disturbance . . . but the soul is almost always in quiet" (IC 7.3.10); "In this
temple of God, in this His dwelling place, He alone and the soul rejoice
together in the deepest silence" (IC 7.3.11).

yielded to the Beloved, in every aspect of being serenely surrendered to his interests and attentive to his messages: "When this impulse comes to you, remember that it comes from this interior dwelling place where God is in our soul, and praise Him very much. For certainly that note or letter is His, written with intense love and in such a way that He wants you alone to understand it and what He asks of you in it. By no means should you fail to respond to His Majesty" (IC 7.3.9). Teresa counsels fidelity to listening to the will of God in the ordinary events of life, whereby the Beloved sends loving messages to the one who lives in continual relationship with him.

Feminine Icons

The images that Teresa presents reveal all her feminine being: as a spouse in love with and completely surrendered to the other, with nothing reserved for herself; and as a sister and fruitful mother concerned with the salvation of souls. She becomes an icon of the feminine face of the church, those women and men in love with the Beloved and capable of surrendering themselves totally to God, fruitful in their apostolic mission. This image is enriched by the feminine biblical figures that characterize these dwelling places, not only at the personal level, but also as models of the church: Martha and Mary (IC 7.1.10; 7.4.12; 7.4.13), where action and contemplation are joined; and Mary Magdalene (IC 7.2.7; 7.4.11), great apostle converted by the unfathomable love of Jesus, to the point of changing her whole life.

In these dwelling places, for the first time in the whole process, Teresa presents a feminine image of God as a mother who sustains life: "Oh, Life of my life! Sustenance that sustains me! . . . For from those divine breasts, where it seems

God is always sustaining the soul there flow streams of milk bringing comfort to all the people of the castle. It seems the Lord desires that in some manner these others in the castle may enjoy the great deal the soul is enjoying and that from that full-flowing river, where this tiny fount is swallowed up, a spurt of that water will sometimes be directed the sustenance of those corporeal things must serve these two who are wed" (IC 7.2.6).[79]

God as mother is an image that speaks of generativity, of comforting, nourishing, sustaining, while taking delight in her child. The relationship with a maternal God, who gives life, care, and strength to the whole person ("all the people of the castle"), makes the good that it does for Teresa's body very explicit, as it is sustained in order to serve. In the fourth dwelling places she had used the image of a child who begins to nurse at its mother's breasts.[80] There its life depended on this food, but in these seventh dwelling places, there is abundance, excess, and giving without measure (the brimming river); there is enjoyment through the life received by those who live these experiences in order to be able to serve. This image also appears in *The Way of Perfection* (W 31.9) and in the *Meditations on the Song of Songs*,[81] where she makes a clear

---

79. "Through some secret aspirations the soul understands clearly that it is God who gives life to our soul" (IC 7.2.6).

80. When all the senses and faculties enter in the interior process she makes allusion to this image of a child who must grow by taking milk at the breast of its mother: "The soul is not yet grown but is like a suckling child. If it turns away from its mother's breasts, what can be expected for it but death?" (IC 4.3.10).

81. In her *Meditations on the Song of Songs*, she uses the image of being sustained by the divine breasts fourteen times.

allusion to the maternal relationship: "It doesn't know what to compare His grace to, unless to the great love a mother has for her child in nourishing and caressing it" (SS 4.4; see also SS 7.9). In all, Teresa has tied the image of mother to generosity, abundance, nurturing, love, and care—features that reveal to us the feminine action of God.

Another new aspect in the seventh dwelling places is the experience of the Trinity. The encounter with the trinitarian mystery is a preparation for the definitive commitment and the graces that would later make Teresa "continuously" live the presence of the Trinity (IC 7.1.7). The relationship of betrothal with Christ has given her the possibility of entering by his hand into the experience of the Trinity.

> When the soul is brought into that dwelling place, the Most Blessed Trinity, all three Persons, through an intellectual vision, is revealed to it through a certain representation of the truth. First there comes an enkindling in the spirit in the manner of a cloud of magnificent splendor; and these Persons are distinct, and through an admirable knowledge the soul understands as a most profound truth that all three Persons are one substance and one power and one knowledge and one God alone. It knows in such a way that what we hold by faith, it understands, we can say, through sight—although the sight is not with the bodily eyes nor with the eyes of the soul, because we are not dealing with an imaginative vision. Here *all three Persons communicate themselves to it, speak to it,* and explain those words of the Lord in the Gospel: that He and the Father and the Holy Spirit will come to dwell with the soul that loves Him and keeps His commandments. (IC 7.1.6; Jn 14:23)

She knows the three Persons by their communication. In one of her accounts she reveals that she knew that all three Persons of the Blessed Trinity were present, and they spoke to her, telling her that from that day, she would improve in three areas. "Each one of these Persons would grant me a favor: one, the favor of charity; another, the favor of being able to suffer gladly; and the third, the favor of experiencing this charity with an enkindling in the soul" (ST 13.1).[82] Each grace received is a distinct expression of love that reveals the way in which each one of the three Persons surrenders itself. We can say that she lived her experience of the Trinity through a feminine perspective, in the sense that she does not present a hierarchy, but rather shows a way of relating and creating communion among the three Persons. Teresa reveals a deep knowledge of the Trinity, beginning with God's loving communication, in a relational communion of mutuality and equality among the three Persons.

A theme that will be developed later is the relationship that exists between the type of communal bonds among the sisters and their experiences of God. Here I simply note a passage that resonates with this experience. She compares heaven, where God dwells,[83] with life in Carmel: "This house is a heaven, if one can be had on this earth" (W 13.7). And the type of communal relationships that she proposes in her reform are those of friendship, mutuality, and equality among sisters, reflecting those in the Trinity: "In this house . . . all must be friends, all must be loved, all must be held dear,

---

82. This testimony, written on May 29, 1571, is the key to the seventh mansions and precedes the experience of the spiritual marriage.

83. "For just as in heaven so in the soul His Majesty must have a room where He dwells alone. Let us call it another heaven" (IC 7.1.3).

all must be helped" (W 4.7). It is a feminine perception of community, where the relations between the sisters are more important than hierarchies, clearly revealing the feminine relational face that she experienced in the Trinity.

In summary, the relationship with Christ in these dwelling places is one of belonging and total giving, which becomes an open and fertile love of humanity, and an intimacy open to life and open to others. The feminine images of spouse, mother, and sister are presented as evident from personal experience and as icons of the life of the church. The inclusion of the image of God as mother catches our attention in a world whose vision of theology is markedly masculine. The emphasis on the images of Martha, Mary, and Mary Magdalene makes her identification with them as a woman clearly explicit, while at the same time highlighting a feminine understanding of action, contemplation, and apostolic ministry. Teresa's trinitarian experience reveals a God who communicates in a loving relationship from a perspective of mutuality and equality in the relationship. In the seventh dwelling places she experiences the constant certainty of the presence of God. The ecstasies and raptures have disappeared; here she lives the relationship with God serenely, having integrated the divine and the human as a woman. Now she herself, through her life transformed in Christ, has become an icon of the humanity of Christ for the church.

7

Toward the Union
of Divine and Human

We focus now on the internal changes that are found in the soul throughout the seven stages of the castle. Since some changes have already been mentioned in discussing the feminine relational dynamic, they will not be repeated here; we have to be aware, however, that the processes are simultaneous.

Overview

In order to have a global sense of the change that is taking place in the soul, we are going to imagine a thread winding continuously throughout the process. This thread, which carries the theme of developing the divine likeness, goes from the first dwelling places to the completion of the seventh. To grow in this divine likeness, Teresa considers the humanity of Christ as the necessary mediation and the way[1] that helps to

---

1. "The Lord Himself says that He is the way; the Lord says also that He is the light and that no one can go to the Father but through Him" (IC 6.7.6).

integrate the human aspect in the process.[2] She presents a way of "Christification," in which the person's humanity, the person's nature, begins orienting itself toward Christ, integrating with the divine, until she becomes like Christ "in whom the divine and the human are joined and who is always that person's companion" (IC 6.7.9). This qualitative transformation into Christ is given by means of the direct relationship of God with the soul,[3] until the person arrives at the union of divine and human within the self and union with Christ in the spiritual marriage. The process also involves some discontinuous elements, which involve those aspects that the person has to leave behind, detach from, and die to, in order to grow.

An overview of the process of integration that the soul experiences can be seen in the following manner. In the first three dwelling places the work consists in reorienting the "natural person" so that the person may be freer, more open to God's action. The fourth dwelling places are ones of transition; the "natural" is still involved as it begins to participate in the experiences of God. The divine likeness is developed through the "supernatural" experiences of relationship with God; these continue transforming the soul until it reaches the union of the human with the divine in the fifth dwelling places; in the sixth and seventh dwelling places, the divine

---

2. "Christ is a very good friend, because we behold Him as man and see Him with weaknesses and trials—and He is company for us. Once we have the habit, it is very easy to find Him present at our side" (L 22.10).

3. Edward Howells makes an interesting analysis and comparison between Teresa of Jesus and John of the Cross, coming to similar conclusions in the different processes: "The mystical is not primarily an experience but a relation . . . which affects our very selfhood." Edward Howells, *John of the Cross and Teresa of Ávila, Spain: Mystical Knowing and Self-hood* (New York: Crossroad, 2002), 1.

likeness is further developed and sharpened while the union of human and divine is strengthened and consolidated.

Reorientation of the "Natural Being"

The process of the reorientation of the natural is found in the first three dwelling places. The soul grows and develops in order to reclaim its own liberty and autonomy, until the truest and most genuine self arises. Teresa, with her strong tendency for connection in friendships and relationships, speaks of a way of detachment from external things and from the self; it consists of a process of separation, differentiation, and allowing the truth about herself to surface. As we have seen (see chapter 6, note 42 in this text), the term "natural" has various synonyms in Teresa's lexicon, such as temperament, feelings, the body, the faculties, what is born of us, and the human.[4] We look now at this way of detachment.

First Dwelling Places

In the first dwelling places, persons are so completely absorbed in exterior things that they cannot hear the Lord calling. Also, "the vassals of the soul" (the faculties: memory, understanding, and will) have little strength (see IC 1.2.12), with the result that the soul does not understand its situation, nor does it have strength of will to make decisions; it finds itself in a state of paralysis.[5] "So, I think, must be the condition of the

---

4.See Tomás Álvarez, ed., *Diccionario de Santa Teresa* (Burgos, Spain: Monte Carmelo, 2002), 196.

5. "Not long ago a very learned man told me that souls who do not practice prayer are like people with paralyzed or crippled bodies" (IC 1.1.6).

soul. Even though it may not be in a bad state, it is so involved in worldly things and so absorbed with its possessions, honor, or business affairs, as I have said, that even though as a matter of fact it would want to see and enjoy its beauty these things do not allow it to; nor does it seem that it can slip free from so many impediments" (IC 1.2.14).

To escape this impasse, Teresa proposes detachment, separation from the exterior: "If a person is to enter the second dwelling places, it is important that he strive to give up unnecessary things and business affairs" (IC 1.2.14).

Second Dwelling Places

In the second dwelling places, the effort to separate from external things allows the soul to "hear" the calls of the Lord;[6] although it wants to respond, it cannot, because bad habits impede it: "But, oh, my Lord and my God, how the whole world's habit of getting involved in vanities vitiates everything! Our faith is so dead that we desire what we see more than what faith tells us. And, indeed, we see only a lot of misfortune in those who go after these visible vanities" (IC 2.1.5).

Here Teresa's proposal is to turn away from the vanities outside the castle (see IC 2.1.5) in order to strengthen the will. Perseverance in such abstinence from self-seeking implies taking the cross as a weapon.[7] Only in this way will the soul be able to separate itself from what binds its will, both internally and externally.

---

6. "So these persons are able to hear the Lord when He calls. Since they are getting closer to where His Majesty dwells . . . from time to time He calls us to draw near Him" (IC 2.1.2).

7. See Rom 6:11–14.

Third Dwelling Places

At this level, individuals have succeeded in detaching themselves from the exterior and can differentiate between the exterior and the interior. Now, however, they risk falling into the temptation of setting themselves up as the point of reference,[8] believing that they have earned their relationship with God[9] through their own works.[10] Such "well-ordered

---

8. Spiritual narcissism can be one of the false solutions or idols that are used in order to avoid the tension caused by the desire to live the ideals and the acceptance of one's own limitations: "On the spiritual level, pseudo-solutions or 'idols' may also be established. There is a kind of search for 'religious experience' that is tantamount to idolatry: making of God an instrument to the fulfillment of one's wishes (Von Balthasar, 1976). Moral narcissism can also be a temptation; it is vividly described in the account of the Pharisee, Luke 18:9-17. Moral narcissism can express itself as legalism, in which case the concern with "rectitude" is the expression of the urge to self-justification rather than of self-transcendence (Demmer, 1976, 31–33, 48)." Bartholomew Kiely, *Psychology and Moral Theology* (Rome: Gregorian University Press, 1987), 210.

9. "They cannot accept patiently that the door of entry to the place where our King dwells be closed to them who consider themselves His vassals" (IC 3.1.6).

10. It seems that Teresa herself made a new pathway in the concept of the gratuitous gift of God. In *The Way of Perfection*, especially in chapters 15, 16, and 17, there is a question in the background that was not completely clarified: does God come to us through virtues or only through grace? "I say that the King of glory will not come to our soul—I mean to be united with it—if we do not make the effort to gain the great virtues" (W 16.6). She also says, "There are souls that God thinks He can win to Himself by these means. Since He sees they are completely lost, His Majesty desires that nothing be wanting on His part. And even though they are in a bad state and lacking in virtue, He gives them spiritual delight, consolation, and tenderness" (W16.8). In *The Way of Perfection* this theme of justification by works is not clearly resolved. It is not until the redaction of the dwelling places that it is developed with more clarity. (See Tomás Álvarez, ed., *Obras completas de Santa Teresa* (Burgos, Spain: Monte Carmelo, 2002), note on W 16.6). The personal experience

souls," believing themselves justified by their works, do a lot of rationalizing, and they may fall into a certain "victimism," thinking that their suffering is through someone else's fault (see IC 3.2.5); or they are scandalized by the faults of others because they have not recognized their own interior poverty.[11] With respect to the body, they are still self-absorbed, not directed toward doing service. They are also held back by fear of bodily suffering and worried about losing their health. "The penance these souls do is well balanced, like their lives. They desire penance a great deal so as to serve our Lord by it. . . . Have no fear that they will kill themselves, for their reason is still very much in control. Love has not yet reached the point of overwhelming reason" (IC 3.2.7).

Teresa explains that the reason for this condition of the souls in the third dwelling places is that they have not yet abandoned themselves (see IC 3.2.9). This lack of detachment from the self means that we must make our way toward the following dwelling places very heavily burdened, "weighed down with this mud of our human misery" (IC 3.2.9). We have to leave those burdens behind so that, traveling light, and freed from ourselves, we can move on to the following dwelling places.

---

of her insignificance, poverty and faults, and the merciful and overwhelming love of God makes her realize that regardless of how many works she performs, there is nothing that justifies the immeasurable love of God for his creatures, who are full of a thousand faults and sins: "The Lord gives [his blessings] when He desires, as He desires and to whom He desires" (IC 4.1.2).God loves us through mercy and without measure. He saves us, redeems, and justifies us through love and not by anything we do.

11. "Let us look at our own faults and leave aside those of others, for it is very characteristic of persons with such well-ordered lives to be shocked by everything" (IC 3.2.13).

The difficulty is solved when these persons learn to put aside their own will, letting go of self and putting the will of God at the center: "In surrendering our will to God in everything, in bringing our life into accordance with what His Majesty ordains for it, and in desiring that His will not ours be done" (IC 3.2.6). At the basis of this qualitative leap is the humble acceptance of one's own truth: "Humility is the ointment for our wounds because if we indeed have humility, even though there may be a time of delay, the surgeon, who is our Lord, will come to heal us" (IC 3.2.6).

In summary, in these first three dwelling places, these persons have tried to free themselves from their own vices and tendencies in order to be disposed to life in Christ. By means of detachment, they pass from a state of no differentiation between the exterior and the interior (in that the body, the senses, and the faculties—absorbed in the exterior—did not have the strength to see or choose) to a state where there is separation and differentiation between the exterior and the interior, enabling them to hear God's calls. Furthermore, those who had been centered on themselves as points of reference are able to pass to a realistic acceptance of their own truth, seeing their own limitations and qualities; this understanding brings them to accept their poverty and put God at the center of their life.[12] Gradually the person enters into the process of recovering the self, in freedom, taking responsibility for his or her own decisions, and is open to recognizing God as Other, different from the self. These persons are becoming involved in a relationship in which they are losing the power of manipulation, recognizing that one cannot use God for one's own

---

12. "Consider yourselves useless servants" (IC 3.1.8).

interest, as an idol. This is done through the humble acceptance of self, of one's own truth, and with the reorientation
of one's body, feelings, and faculties. All their "natural being"
now tends toward the search for and the encounter with God,
so that they now live in greater harmony and are more disposed to respond to the call that is found in the depths of
their beings.

Putting Together the Human and the Divine

Here "putting together the human and divine" refers to an
internal ordering that is a prelude to the full integration that
takes place in later dwelling places.

Fourth Dwelling Places

In this stage "the natural and the supernatural are joined" (IC
4.3.14). It deals with a type of prayer relationship, as we have
already seen, in which Teresa distinguishes consolations (*contentos*) and delights (*gustos*). Let us look at the characteristics
of the soul in respect to each of them.

Consolations (contentos)

The consolations "have their beginning in our own human
nature and end in God" (IC 4.1.4). In this type of prayer
the activities of the imagination and the will help to distinguish the person's situation. Teresa's imagination, active and
completely feminine, leads to many conflicts: "Terrible trials are suffered because we don't understand ourselves, and
that which isn't bad at all but good we think is a serious
fault. . . . But the soul is perhaps completely joined with

Him in the dwelling places very close to the center while the mind is on the outskirts of the castle suffering from a thousand wild poisonous beasts" (IC 4.1.9).

The imagination may stir up many of the "poisonous beasts" from the first dwelling places: the day's events, memories from the past, the emotional tug of war of relationships.[13] The desire to fight with the imagination generates a wearisome battle because we find no rest within ourselves, which proves to be "very painful and almost unbearable" (see IC 4.1.12; 4.1.13). Furthermore, the feminine tendency to remain in connection with the exterior also plays a part in the imagination; specific activities, people, and relationships will appear through the imagination. Then what is there to do? Teresa suggests accepting these journeys of the imagination as part of our human limitation, like eating and sleeping, without excusing it (see IC 4.1.11) and letting the chatter go on (see IC 4.1.13). Despite the presence of the *contentos*, some parts of the individual's emotional and affective elements are not yet fully engaged in the relationship with God.

In the will, the person's interests are also mixed. Since *contentos* begin with us, the solace they bring bears with it some of our sensuality (see IC 4.1.5): "They are sometimes mixed with

---

13. What Teresa calls imagination are those thoughts and images that come without our seeking them and that have to do with the unconscious and with the affective and emotional life. They come more easily with fatigue, and are usually persistent, continuing on their own, seeking gratification, not allowing a space of silence for prayer. The imagination and the thoughts that come spontaneously are usually an excellent field of investigation that reveals many aspects of the person. The fact that these thoughts continue to interfere with prayer may indicate that the affective and emotional areas are entangled in interests other than the relationship with God. But such distractions, however, may also be primarily due to the person's deep fatigue.

our own passions" (IC 4.2.1), and they can manifest bodily effects. The result is that "the consolation comes through our own efforts," making noise (see IC 4.2.3) because our "natural being" tends to seek consolation and wants to keep it for itself. When *contentos* arise in this prayer, they can have a selfish desire as a second objective; Teresa calls such desires weaknesses and deals with them from the feminine perspective in the sixth dwelling places. Either through the imagination or through the will, in the consolations "the natural" continues as slave of one's tendencies and desires as much at the affective-emotional level as at the perceptive-cognitive level.

Spiritual Delights (Gustos)

The "spiritual delights (*gustos*) begin in God, but our human nature feels and enjoys them" (IC 4.1.4). The author describes three consequences of this "supernatural" action, direct from God: As has already been said in chapter 6, all that is human is included in the divine experience, in the relationship that transforms, involving the whole person.[14] This inclusion in turn provokes an "expansion or dilation of the soul,"[15] "*cum dilataste cor meum*" [Ps 119:32. "For you open my docile heart"; literally, "you make my heart broad." *New American Bible*, Catholic World Press, 1987] (IC 4.1.5). Also, in these

---

14. "When He is pleased to grant some supernatural favor—He produces this delight with the greatest peace and quiet and sweetness in the very interior part of ourselves. . . . Afterward the delight fills everything; this water overflows through all the dwelling places and faculties until reaching the body" (IC 4.2.4).

15. "What an expansion or dilation of the soul is may be clearly understood from the example of a fount whose water doesn't overflow into a stream because the fount itself is constructed of such material that the more water there is flowing into it the larger the trough becomes" (IC 4.3.9).

dwelling places the soul begins a new way of knowing that culminates in the sixth mansions.[16] This new knowledge does not come from the usual way of reasoning: "Through the work of the senses and faculties she couldn't in any way or in a thousand years understand what she understands here in the briefest time" (IC 5.4.4); rather, it is a knowledge that comes directly from God: "When His Majesty desires the intellect to stop, He occupies it in another way and gives it a light so far above what we can attain that it remains absorbed. Then, without knowing how, the intellect is much better instructed than it was through all the soul's efforts not to make use of it" (IC 4.3.6).

With these changes in the soul, the process of uniting the divine and the human is initiated, a process that will be developed in the dwelling places to follow.

Fifth Dwelling Places

Teresa now presents two principal ideas in these dwelling places, based on the image of the metamorphosis of the silkworm into a butterfly: death that leads to new life. We will see what this death involves, and how its new life will be.

Death

The death of the worm represents all the losses that the soul has experienced throughout the process, in separating from

---

16. In the dynamic of knowing, there are "two cognitive moments": one is a more habitual type of knowing, which tends to be repeated and is somewhat more automatic; a second type is more conscious, more focused, and more active, direct, and intentional. See Franco Imoda, *Sviluppo Umano, Psicología e Mistero* (Casale Monferrato, Italy: Piemme, 1993), 237–38. Here Teresa refers to a new way of knowing that comes from God and begins to give her a new vision of things.

the exterior and in humbly accepting its own limits and defects, as well as its own positive characteristics.[17] These losses require separation from self, implying the death of self-love and self-esteem (see IC 5.3.6).[18]

New Life

In its new life, the worm has changed from delights and desires, for "it now has wings" (IC 5.2.8) and "doesn't recognize itself" (IC 5.2.7). Before, it was afraid of suffering, but now it is strong and courageous; it was attached to many people and things that now weary it (see IC 5.2.8). This new life of the soul continues being developed in these and in the following dwelling places. The affections become ordered as a result of the soul's relationship with Christ. In the intimate encounter with God in prayer, "God brought her into the wine cellar and put charity in order within her" (IC 5.2.12). From this encounter, love of neighbor is born from the center of the soul.[19] The soul is "impressed with His seal"

---

17. When people do not reject the negative aspects of the self, but recognize their own truth, they can come to integrate positive and negative aspects of themselves, creating cohesion in the self . Thanks to the love they have felt, they are able to incorporate the good image and the bad image of themselves as part of their own reality, integrating aspects that are cognitive, affective, volitional, interpersonal, and behavioral. See Imoda, *Sviluppo*, 301–4.

18. She refers here to the death of the self that is centered in itself.

19. In her book *Meditations on the Song of Songs*, Teresa says, referring to the phrase, "She (the bride) says *He brought me into the wine cellar; set charity in order within me*, she understands . . . to one He gives a little wine of devotion, to another more, with another He increases it in such a way that the person begins to go out from himself, from his sensuality, and from all earthly things; to some He gives great fervor in His service; to others, impulses of love; to others, great charity toward their neighbors. These gifts are given in such a way that these persons go about so stupefied they do not feel the great

(IC 5.2.12), the seal of love; now the soul goes forth from this union marked with love of God and love of neighbor. A new life is born through the letting go of self, and revealed in the unity of love of God and love of neighbor. The encounter of the divine with the human continues forming a new person, more like Christ. Now she loves others with the same love with which she is loved, making Christ present among his sisters and brothers.

Sixth Dwelling Places

The qualitative changes that take place in those who have arrived at the "betrothal" with God involve the cognitive, affective, and relational areas; they now unite the human and the divine.

A New Way of Knowing

A new way of knowing reality is now established and extended,[20] beginning with a higher knowledge of the greatness and the truths of God,[21] so that without understanding how, all knowledge is already found within the self (see L 27.8).

---

trials that take place here" (SS 6.3). Later, regarding the expression "The King set charity in order in me," she continues: "Set it in order so well that the love the soul had for the world is taken away; the soul's love of itself turns to disregard; its love for its relatives is such that it loves them solely for God; its love for its neighbors and its enemies is unbelievable unless experienced—a very strong love; its love of God is boundless, for sometimes the love impels it so much that its lowly nature cannot endure the love" (SS 6.13).

20. What had been initiated in the fourth mansions is now further strengthened, a new way of knowing that goes beyond appearance.

21. We could now call this qualitative leap the development of the "cognitive self." Not a development found in normal growth, it is acquired by a relationship with God that we consider as a personal relationship; therefore the new knowledge comes from a faith perspective.

The encounter with the Wisdom of God gives the soul, on the one hand, a new vision of the world, of itself, and of the human person; and, on the other hand, an attitude of adoration,[22] born of the knowledge of God.

Experience of the Humanity of Christ

The experience of the humanity of Christ that she relates in these dwelling places *heals the memory*. The *affective memory* is the emotional residue of the person's most significant experiences, a kind of live documentation of the history of the person's whole emotional life, at times unconscious but alive and active.[23] The affective memory creates a certain predisposition to react to or relive a past emotion, positive or negative, when a situation arises that is either actually or symbolically similar to a past one. These predispositions are characteristics that appear in the tendencies of the personality, written into the person's family and cultural history. In Teresa's narration in *The Book of Her Life*, we see how she was healed of her tendencies imprinted in the affective memory by means of the humanity of Christ.

Consolidation

This new way of knowing and loving from the experience of her relationship with God is proven under trial: even in

---

22. "Some truths about the grandeur of God remain so fixed in this soul, that even if faith were not to tell it who God is and of its obligation to believe that He is God, from that very moment it would adore Him as God" (IC 6.4.6).

23. It was Magda Arnold who reported this concept to psychology. See Magda B. Arnold, *Emotion and Personality* (New York: Columbia University Press, 1960).

intense experiences of the absence of God, she manages to maintain a *constant relationship of loving*. That is, her love of God is independent of her experience of God's presence or absence.[24] She remains in love, whether she experiences loneliness or feels God's company.

Toward Union

As the bond with Christ is strengthened, so is the drive toward unity between the human and the divine. Teresa identifies fleeing from the humanity of Christ as a false kind of "spiritual evasion": a certain resistance to accepting the passion[25] as well as human suffering, and a lack of humility (L 22.5) in refusing to accept human limitations. She invites us to see Christ resurrected and glorious but without being separated from his humanity, because he is the true friend[26] and the sure way to the Father.[27] Almost all the visions that she has of him are of the resurrected Christ, revealing the

---

24. Here we see characteristics similar to what psychology refers to as "object constancy", wherein the person can maintain a continuous relationship with an object perceived cognitively and affectively, whether it is still present or not. See Otto Kernberg, *Object Relations Theory and Clinical Psychoanalysis* (New York: Aronson, 1976), 64–79.

25. It could also be the case that the excessive emphasis put on the passion of Christ in Teresa's day overshadowed the fact that Jesus had conquered death and pain through his resurrection.

26. "Whoever lives in the presence of so good a friend and excellent a leader, who went ahead of us to be the first to suffer, can endure all things. The Lord helps us, strengthens us, and never fails; He is a true friend" (L 22.6).

27. "For if they lose the guide, who is the good Jesus, they will not hit upon the right road. . . . The Lord Himself says that He is the way; the Lord says also that He is the light and that no one can go to the Father but through Him" (IC 6.7.6).

unity of his divine and human mystery. Christ is the mediator, the bridge that permits the union with the divinity by means of his humanity united to ours.[28] Without Christ we would remain far from God.

To summarize, *the union of the human with the divine begins with* the supernatural action of God, starting with the fourth dwelling places. The first step is the participation of the human in the divine with the inclusion of the senses, the faculties, and the body. This experience increases the person's capacity for a deeper relationship with God. The relationship with the humanity of Christ puts the affections in order and heals the affective memory in such a way that it enables persons to love in God's way, as they are loved. A new way of knowing from God's wisdom now begins, changing the person's vision of life and the world. This new mode of loving and knowing is strengthened and reinforced in the trials of the absences of God (see Teresa's experience of hell, L 32.1), in which the person remains faithful in the darkness, continuously in loving relationship with God. Persons in these dwelling places give testimony to God's life in them; the human has drawn close to the divine.

Divine and Human Together

Because of the divine and human union found in the center of the soul, there is a change that restructures the person. The concept of the "center of the soul" has already been introduced in the previous chapter. In the center of the soul God dwells, together with the spirit of the soul. Teresa calls our

---

28. Teresa constantly insists on the union of the divinity and humanity of Christ that comes to her from the apparitions of Him as risen, with the signs of the passion, showing Him as human and God.

attention to the fact that this "depth" or "center" of the soul coincides with the spirit of the soul itself because, in her opinion, "there is a certain difference between the soul and the spirit, although the soul is all one" (introduction to IC 7.1).

Seventh Dwelling Places

For the process of transformation in Christ, the soul becomes more and more like God, through the Son. In Teresian symbolism, that signifies that the soul is getting closer and closer to its center, where God is, and to its own spirit, formed in the image of God: "The essential part of her soul never moved from that room" (IC 7.1.10). Only God can bring it to this dwelling place, however, and bring about this leap to the union of the spiritual matrimony: "He brings it [this soul], before the spiritual marriage is consummated, into His dwelling place which is this seventh. For just as in heaven so in the soul His Majesty must have a room where He dwells alone. Let us call it another heaven" (IC 7.1.3).

There in the center of the soul,[29] Teresa has the trinitarian experience, and the marriage union with Christ is now accomplished: "This secret union takes place in the very interior center of the soul" (IC 7.2.3). The whole human nature of the person has been becoming "Christified"; it unites in the "very, very interior" with Christ himself. The union of the human and divine is made possible in her through the fullness of similarity with Christ, and by the union of her entire person with the human and divine Christ.

---

29. "The symbol permits Teresa to locate in the center of the soul the deepest dimension of the human 'I', and at the same time the presence of the divine, and the consummation of the union between the two." Álvarez, *Diccionario*, 141.

Teresa reveals to us that she has encountered her most profound identity as a woman in discovering the image of Christ in her own soul. She has seen the *original image* of herself, and she perceives it reflected in her own life; like Paul of Tarsus, she can say that her life is now Christ (IC 7.2.5). Like him she is no longer afraid of death or suffering because of being with Christ as He is seen in the mirror that she contemplates where her image is sculpted (see IC 7.2.8). She believes that God grants these graces to make the life of Christ possible in us (see IC 7.4.4).

This qualitative leap in the process implies that as a woman, Teresa fully lives her identity as an image of God in the totality of her human person. She lives the union of the human and the divine in a form similar to that of Christ. For her, however, as for any one of us, this is a grace that can be lost; for Christ this union is unwavering and constant, forming part of his identity as Word Incarnate.

In that same context the symbolism of Martha and Mary reappears to explain that by this union, action and contemplation are no longer divided as before, when Martha was worried about duties and Mary stayed absorbed in the presence of the Lord.[30] After the spiritual marriage, Martha and Mary are together: "Believe me, Martha and Mary must join together

---

30. "In everything she found herself improved, and it seemed to her, despite the trials she underwent and the business affairs she had to attend to, that the essential part of her soul never moved from that room. As a result, it seemed to her that there was, in a certain way, a division in her soul. And while suffering some great trials a little after God granted her this favor, she complained of that part of the soul, as Martha complained of Mary, and sometimes pointed out that it was there always enjoying that quietude at its own pleasure while leaving her in the midst of so many trials and occupations that she could not keep it company" (IC 7.1.10).

in order to show hospitality to the Lord and have Him always present and not host Him badly by failing to give Him something to eat. How would Mary, always seated at His feet, provide Him with food if her sister did not help her? His food is that in every way possible we draw souls that they may be saved and praise Him always" (IC 7.4.12).

Through this marriage, there is an experience of "continuity" of the Lord's presence,[31] which fortifies the person's desire to keep living and surrendering the body, senses, faculties, and the whole person to the service of the kingdom. There is much more apostolic action than before, and in the middle of it lives the presence of God (IC 7.1.8).

In summary, the experience of the union of divine and human in the seventh dwelling places is that the person becomes more and more like Christ until God unites the person's own spirit, made in the image of God, with Christ. Thus the process reaches completion when they have become like Christ in all of their own humanity, achieving the fullness of their identity as an image of God; they are men and women, living images of him. This union integrates these persons' lives of action and contemplation, making their actions spring from the most profound center of their beings.

---

31. "It turns and looks within itself and at how continually it experiences His presence, and with that it is content and offers His Majesty the desire to live as the most costly offering it can give Him" (IC 7.3.7).

8

Teresian Contributions to Psychology, Mysticism, and Prophecy

To conclude the reading of Teresa's spiritual journey from the perspective of feminine relationships, we want to touch on her contributions to psychology, mysticism and prophecy, not just for her own time, but for today as well. We can say that Teresa of Jesus is a living memory for the church. For all women of faith, her life and spiritual development are a profound call to live the mystical and prophetic dimensions in today's world. She is an icon of the church as a bride and, at the same time, an icon of Christ surrendered lovingly to the service of humankind. *The Interior Castle* supports a feminine spirituality that involves a pedagogic process of growth and appropriation of the identity of women. In it, Teresa develops her feminine relational capacity to every level, committing herself to the church and to society, beginning with a process of liberation from the sociocultural conditioning that impeded revealing the face of Christ in her being as a woman. Her spirituality is full of life, mysticism, prophecy, and a radical commitment to God, a gift for both women and men who want to give their lives to form the living body of Christ today.

One of the limitations in this investigation has been Teresa's historical distance from our century, since the situation of today's woman is very different from that of the sixteenth century. This distance is also an advantage, however, in that it helps to identify constants that have persisted throughout history. The conclusions of this investigation invite us to reread her spirituality from the feminine perspective.

Feminine Process of Becoming Whole: Human and Divine Maturation

The term *whole* refers here to the entire person, in all one's physical, mental, emotional, human, and divine aspects. The experience lived by Teresa of Jesus throughout the dwelling places gives us a vision of an integrative process that involves the whole person. The point of departure is the recovery of Teresa's own dignity and identity as a woman, the image of God in Christ. Her transformation to a likeness of Christ, as a concrete and historical person is the common thread of the entire process. As she advances, the integration is extended to include all the dimensions of her life as a woman: her body; her feminine way of feeling and loving; her options, actions, experiences, and relationships; her way of being, in the culture of her time, a free woman. All is integrated until she becomes like Christ. In short, this process is the result of Teresa's life involved in friendship with Christ and her collaboration in his work of redemption.

The unity and integration of this experience has been possible because Teresa herself has known and experienced what it is to know and experience God. She has made herself the subject of this experience, appropriating it as her own. Through discernment she has distinguished between the experience of self and the experience of God, that is, the truth of self and the truth of God. Through her relationship with God she achieved her identity of fullness of woman in Christ. This process of integration implies progressive stages of growth that we can chart in the following way.

Table of Stages of Growth toward Totality in Teresa of Jesus

Dwelling places	Structural changes in the person[1]
First	No differentiation between external and internal Relationship with God defined very little
Second	Differentiation between external and internal Begins to hear the calls of God
Third	Good self-image, to the extent of taking self as point of reference (a form of narcissism of complacent souls) Realistic acceptance of self; emergence of a more genuine and true self Recognition of the diversity of the Other Feeling loved, accepted, and redeemed with one's own limits and defects. Love of gratitude is born.
Fourth	Still no integration of the whole person; imagination and the will go their own way. An interior expansion that involves aspects of the person that were outside of the relationship.

Continued

---

1. See chapter 5 in this text for a discussion of structural aspects.

Continued

Dwelling places	Structural changes in the person
Fifth	The affect is ordered. Person is totally in love and surrendered to love. Goes out of self in loving service Entire person is in relationship with God.
Sixth	A new way of knowing and loving Healing of memory and of its affective-relational dynamic Consolidation of a loving relationship in spite of the experiences of solitude, the absences of God, and others
Seventh	Integration and union of the divine and the human Lives what it was desiring to live Coherence between the ideal and the reality Lives in serenity and open to a universal love Experience of the continual presence of the love of God

What can we conclude from this feminine process toward integration?

The fundamental key that unlocks the development of human and divine maturation is the relational aspect. As a woman, Teresa tends to live the relational aspect in greater unity and integration with her affectivity, corporality, and sexuality. This is also true in her relations with others and with Christ. In order to really follow Jesus, both women and men must move toward the final maturation of becoming the likeness of Christ. Yet the process of becoming Christ has a different path for men and women because femininity in the relational process displays more connection and empathy while masculinity manifests less. This indicates that the feminine and masculine are distinct "modes," or "ways," in the relationship; however, at the level of content—in growth and in human and divine maturation—they have the same end. So we can say there are differences between male and female in the way of relating and of being in the world but not in the essential process of transformation in Christ.

From the psychological point of view, the relationship with God is a structural element of human maturation.[2] We can say this because the changes of the soul that Teresa presents in *The Interior Castle* show some points in common with the stages of structural development of the self of Otto Kernberg in his object relations theory.[3] I will point out only some differences and similarities between them, since in order to establish a bridge of methodological dialogue between these authors, further investigation would be necessary.[4]

---

2. See Massimo Diana, *Ciclo di vita ed esperienza religiosa* (Bologna, Italy: Edizioni Dehoniana Bologna, 2004).

3. The theory of object relations deals with the primary relations in those that form representations of the parental figures. These representations of early infancy influence relationships throughout the length of life in an unconscious way. They are called object relations because the psychoanalytic tradition has used the term "object" to refer to internal representations of the person. I agree, however, with Otto Kernberg, one of the representatives of this theory, who suggests changing the term to "human object," corresponding to the use of this term in dealing with relationships with others in analytical metapsychology. Otto Kernberg, *Object Relations Theory and Clinical Psychoanalysis* (New York: Aronson, 1976), 58.

4. The dialogue between the theory of Kernberg and the Teresian experience sheds light and helps us value human maturity as brought about through religious experience.

Stages of Development of the Self in Kernberg[5]

Stage	Structural changes of the self
Autism	Undifferentiated state Begins to develop the representation of the self and of the object The relationship is not well defined; there is fusion.
Symbiosis	There is differentiation of the object and the image of the self, with a good, stable internal representation of object-self. A fragmented self; lives in symbiosis The physical confines begin to be marked.
Differentiation	Internal differentiation of the good nuclear representation Differentiation of self and of the object in the bad nuclear representation At the end of this stage there is an integration of the good and bad representations of the object in whole object representations. A grandiose or vulnerable self At the relational level, differentiation of self and object
Integration of the image of self	A more coherent self is formed, although still rigid. The concept of the self is consolidated, and the object representations increase the affective capacities. Representations of the self and idealized objects appear. Psychic structures of a superior level are developed. Permanence of the object is found in the relationship.

Continued

---

5. Kernberg, *Object Relations Theory*, 58–76.

Continued

Stage	Structural changes of the self
Consolidation of intrapsychic structures of superior level	A positive, flexible, and stable ego is consolidated, constructed around the dynamic relationship or by the integration between what the individual is and what she or he is called to be, between the actual self and the ideal self (between the ego and the superego). A harmonious world of interiorized object representations constitutes an internal scope of continuous growth that gives love, confirmation, support, and guidance within the relations of the self. This internal world in turn grants a new dimension to interaction with others. There is constancy of the loved object in the relationship.

In writing *The Interior Castle*, Teresa of Jesus was describing a path of relationship with God, not a psychological process. As has already been mentioned, however, the relationship with God is a real process of the whole person that implies the structural transformation of the person in every area of life. We can distinguish two diverse horizons: Kernberg is concerned with the relations at a psychosocial and intrapsychic level, while Teresa establishes the relationship with God in a horizon of theocentric auto-transcendence, with consequences in the psychosocial and intrapsychic horizon. The point of dialogue between the two is established from the relational perspective.

Kernberg presents the structural development of the self from the perspective of psychotherapeutic treatment with adults, taking into account the conscious and the unconscious derived from representations formed in early infancy. His objective is to help people unblock aspects of their past lives that impede mature relationships and to guide them in restructuring themselves interiorly.

Teresa of Jesus, on the other hand, presented a process of maturation of the image and likeness of God, by means of the relationship with the humanity of Christ, in which the human person and the divine image are both developed until becoming transformed in Christ. Teresa did not take into account aspects of the unconscious, since those concepts were unknown in the sixteenth century. She does, however, call our attention to "states of the soul" and human behaviors that can block growth in the relationship with God; she identifies "well-behaved souls," "weaknesses," "melancholies," and "pusillanimity" as attitudes to overcome in the relational process.

With this process we confirm that in the experience she lived, Teresa overcame the dichotomy between nature and grace presented by the theology of her time. It was not until the twentieth century that a new theological vision of the unity of nature and grace was proposed by Karl Rahner, who refused to separate the world of the supernatural—"there, distant"—and the lower world of nature in the "here and now." Rahner considered grace as originating from God, but he did not separate its efficacy from daily life, nor from psychic life, whether conscious or unconscious. He described the human person as gifted with a capacity for self-transcendence, experiencing the intangible and incomprehensible mystery of God in our history in the human personality. In this sense, human history is not only the concrete place where God is revealed, but it must also be the primary field of interest of theological reflection.[6]

---

6. Karl Rahner, *Theologian of the Graced Search for Meaning*, ed. Geffrey B. Kelly (Minneapolis: Fortress Press, 1992), 39. See also Ana Maria Rizzuto, "Processi psicodinamici nella vita religiosa e spirituale," *Tredimensioni* 3 (2006): 10–30.

Another point to consider is the concept of the self in these authors. Teresa referred to the term *soul*, understanding it as the fixed, permanent part of the identity of the person throughout all the processes of transformation and change in the relationship with God. Kernberg, in contrast, proposes that in the relationship with its mother, beginning with the symbiotic phase, the baby enters into the phase of differentiation or individuation, in which stable limits are being configured;[7] from there the self emerges in an experience of self-knowing, with a relative stability that persists by a principal of continuity.[8] In both processes the self emerges and is consolidated as the fruit of relationship, and persists in continuity.

We add that the psychoanalytic contribution of Ana-Maria Rizzuto on the relationship with God from the perspective of object relations can mediate between the autotranscendent and psychosocial horizons, inasmuch as it considers the "object representations" of God.[9] In fact, in Teresa's journey, we note

7. Otto Kernberg, *Aggression in Personality Disorders and Perversions* (New Haven, Conn.: Yale University Press, 1992), 17.

8. Kernberg, 98.

9. Ana-Maria Rizzuto, *The Birth of the Living God* (Chicago: University of Chicago Press, 1979). In this book the author analyzes the characteristics of the image of God that every human being forms in the first years of life. Rizzuto investigates the influence of relationships with parents, society, culture, and crises in each stage of life in the formation of this image. She speaks of an "object representation" of God as a psychic entity internalized in a cultural and social context that represents God and the relationship with Him. This psychoanalytic concept is clearly distinguished from the idea of God. It deals with an image formed, beginning with the image of the parents and the image of the self, and structured by means of a complex process of memories that are emotive-affective, perceptive, symbolic, sensory-motor, and later conceptual and intellectual. The structuring is such that a relationship that matures with

how the image of God evolves as the relationship with Christ grows deeper. Beginning with a distant image, in a relationship of inequality, it is transformed into a relationship of mutuality and parity with Christ in the betrothal.[10]

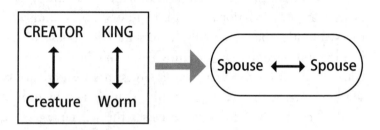

From a relationship of inequality   to a relationship of mutuality

From all the above we can conclude the following:

- From the feminine perspective, while acknowledging that each individual walks a unique road that cannot be compared to those of others, the relational process in the works of Teresa of Jesus is existential and progressive; it involves the totality of the person and is entirely involved with the dynamic of human maturation.

- The recovery of the feminine in spirituality implies a relational perspective of connection and empathy that assumes

the parents, together with other persons in a sociocultural context, would also involve a mature relationship with God. In contrast, an immature and sometimes negative relationship with the parents would affect the "representation" that persons form of God and their relationship with him. The process of religious maturation implies coming closer and closer to the God that Jesus reveals to us in the Gospel.

10. See Mary Frohlich, *The Intersubjectivity of the Mystic* (Atlanta: Scholars Press, 1993).

its own human nature in relationship with oneself, with God, and with others.

• Considering the relational perspective, this question arises: is the road of prayer and the relationship with Christ a proposal for human growth, and integration with the divine image? Did Teresa live what in today's language might be called a Christotherapy? It seems that she did, and that from her vision, the relationship with the human and divine Christ constitutes the way of Christian maturation for believers; although the concrete process may look quite different for each person, that core relationship is essential.

Mystical Experience: Openness to Relationship with a Third Person

When Teresa of Jesus was proclaimed a Doctor of the Church, one of the most compelling aspects of her teaching was the knowledge of the mystery of Christ and the consequences that this had in her life: Teresa embodied the "divinization of the human and the humanization of the divine."[11] The humanity of Christ was the fundamental mediation in this process.

To deepen our understanding of the union of the divine and human that Teresa lived, the psychoanalytic concept of "transitional space" can shed some light.[12] In psychoanalytic

---

11. "Sancta Teresia a Iesu Doctor Ecclesiae," *Ephemerides Carmeliticae* 21 (1970): 1–3.

12. I am inspired by the concept of transitional objects, the intermediate area of experience, in Donald Winnicott's "Transitional Objects and Transitional Phenomena," *International Journal of Psychoanalysis* 34, no. 2 (1953): 89–97. According to Winnicott, this experience, which includes both inner and outer reality, begins in infancy and remains a significant influence in creative areas such as art and religion throughout the person's life.

terms, we can say that the experience of her relationship with the humanity of Christ permits an intermediate space of dialogue between her own humanity, which belongs to her and which she conceives of subjectively, and the humanity of Christ, which also belongs to her and is united to the divinity. This humanity shared by both Christ and Teresa is at the same time shared by all humankind. The relationship between them creates a common intermediate space open to external reality and at the same time is present in the internal reality. A similar relationship takes place from the perspective of the union of the divine in Teresa with the Trinity.

The process of change at the cognitive, affective, and structural levels of Teresa's being is rooted in her relationship with Christ; it is this relationship that makes possible the human-divine union within her person, with openness both toward humanity and toward the Trinity. The following schematic represents this process.

As we have seen, through her relationship with Christ, Teresa constructs a meaning to help her integrate the union of the human and the divine. Nevertheless, for Teresa this experience begins with division, not integration, as she struggles to try to harmonize the world and God (see L 7.17). The temptation Teresa faced was to propose a false solution to living out this dialectic by avoiding the human and distancing herself from the humanity of Christ. She vacillated between a "platonic" concept of the person, woven in the spirituality and dominant culture of her time, where the body, and above all her woman's body, with its affect, feelings, and faculties, was considered base and less worthy of the divinity. As a woman, however, she also had an innate tendency to live out her bodily aspects in unity

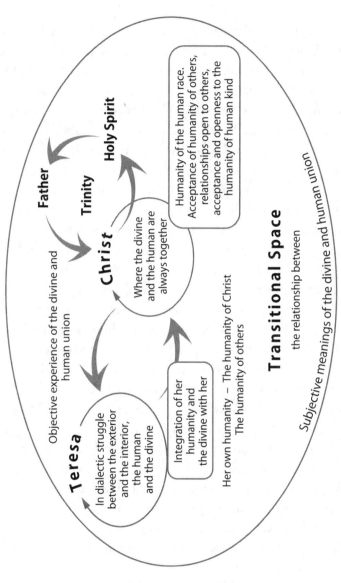

Relationship with the humanity of Christ open to the Trinity and to our sisters and brothers

and integration, a characteristic that was surely enriched by her Jewish roots.[13]

Through her relationship with the humanity of Christ, Teresa embraces her human condition. This opens her to solidarity with all humankind, with whom she shares the same condition. At the same time it also opens her to the Trinity, whose image she bears within. It is in relationship with the humanity of Christ that Teresa re-creates, elaborates, and assembles the meaning of her own humanity, orienting it to the development of the divine likeness. Through the human Christ, she takes upon herself all that is related to the materiality of life as it is: the active life, the external aspects of her person, her woman's body, her sensitivity, the feminine way of feeling, the imagination, and her way of loving, understanding, and relating. Ultimately, Teresa integrates all of her human experience and its reality in the divine likeness.

On accepting her own humanity in Christ, Teresa is simultaneously opened—to others, to humanity, and to the divinity—while weaving the love of God and neighbor into the same process. Being welcomed in her humanity as a woman, she can welcome the humanity of others, especially of her sisters. Compassion opens Teresa to the world of suffering and of the poor: "It seems to me I have much more compassion for the poor than I used to. I feel such great pity and desire to find relief for them that if it were up to me I would give them the clothes off my back. I feel no repugnance whatsoever toward them, toward speaking to or touching them. This I now see is a gift given by God. For even though I used to give alms for love of Him, I didn't have the natural

---

13. In the Old Testament the human person is conceived of as one, with no separation of body and soul.

compassion" (ST 2.4, written in 1562, probably in Toledo, and surely directed to Father Pedro Ibáñez).

On the other hand, on opening herself to the indwelling Trinity and in union with Christ, she reclaims her own feminine being in God, finding in him characteristics that reveal to us the feminine action of God (see the section titled "Feminine Icons" in chapter 6 of this text). We can draw several conclusions from these aspects of the process, which we will explore below.

Teresa Lives the Mystery of the Incarnation

In her mystical relationship with the humanity of Christ, Teresa lives the mystery of the incarnation; Christ is united to her woman's humanity in solidarity with all the human race (see GS 22).

The Intrinsic Goodness of Being a Woman

By means of her relationship with the humanity of Christ, Teresa reclaims the intrinsic goodness of her being a woman and the value of the feminine body in reference to God. In her relationship with Christ, she includes the participation of the body in sufferings and illnesses, and also in pleasures, such as those of the mystical experiences. (See her joys when the theme of the betrothal is dealt with, in IC 5 and 6.)

Transformation in Christ

God is present in the historical conditioning of Teresa of Jesus. She is redeemed and transformed in Christ precisely in her physical, psychological, and spiritual being as a woman. This transformation includes aspects of gender and capacity but goes beyond those. The particulars of the historical Jesus, such as his gender, race, and any other specific details, do not signify that God is incarnated more in these realities than in others. The incarnation is universal: "For by His incarnation the Son of God has united Himself in some fashion with every man" (GS 22). It is understood that here *man* means everyone, thus including the humanity of all human beings in their historical particulars. In Teresa's case, her humanity and her bodily reality as a woman enter into a process of *Christification* until she shares with Christ the dynamic inner life of the Persons of the Trinity.

Bearing the Image of Christ

As a woman, Teresa is a bearer of the image of Christ by participation in the mysteries of his life and by her transformation in him. Within her we witness the reality St. Paul describes: "We are being transformed into that same image each time more glorious" (2 Cor 3:18), or in Teresa's own words, "We see in that mirror that we contemplate where our image is sculpted" (IC 7.2.8). In her human transformation, Teresa becomes in history a living extension of Christ's own humanity.

The Transformation Continues

By Teresa's union with Christ, the feminine has continued becoming transformed into the divine in her.[14] With Mary, Teresa, and other holy women, "We do know that when it is revealed we shall be like him, for we shall see him as he is" (1 Jn 3:2).

---

14. "For, since Christ died for all men and . . . the ultimate vocation of man is in fact one, and divine" (GS 22). (We understand the terms *men* and *man* to be used inclusively.)

The Prophetic Dimension of Teresa's Life

Her relationship with God freed Teresa from the sociocultural conditioning that had kept her from fulfilling her fundamental call to be fully a woman in Christ.[15] She proposed a theological anthropology whereby men and women have the same dignity, where both are images and likenesses of God and both are called to be images of Christ. Moreover, moved by her desire to "save souls," Teresa questioned the impossibility of playing a public role as a woman in the church. Through her relationship with Christ she was also liberated from a false idealization of men, from the submission to and affective dependence on them that was encouraged by the cultural concept of woman in her time, as well as by her own personality and conditioning. Finally, we can see that finding the truth in her relationship with God liberated Teresa from placing her security in the truth of the "lettered" (the cultured and learned). She experienced that "He alone is Truth that cannot lie," and she acknowledged "what David says in a psalm about every man being a liar" (IC 6.10.5). Real truth and wisdom go far beyond knowing things, receiving instruction, or possessing only some truths.

We can conclude that initially Teresa passed through a personal liberation from her own sociocultural conditioning and that, later in the Carmelite reform, she developed and presented a manner of living that would become the leaven of a social and ecclesial transformation that has continued even into our day. Her prophetic role as a woman in the church thus remains alive and current. Like Mary in the Magnificat, Teresa recognized the reality of her own insignificance and

---

15. "And put on the new self, created in God's way in righteousness and holiness of truth" (Eph 4:24).

marginalization because she was a woman and she asked God to let her see his power at work in the world's *anawim*, his poor and little ones. "Let Your grandeur appear in a creature so feminine and lowly, whatever the cost to her, so that the world may know that this grandeur is not hers at all and may praise You" (IC 6.6.4).

Relationships among Women

Through our journey through *The Interior Castle* we discover some inferences about the relationships among women in the works of Teresa of Jesus.[16] As a woman, from her feminine identity, she shows other women, especially her nuns, a process of socialization and formation on the road of spiritual growth. Teresa writes for them because they understand each other well, and she takes feminine characteristics into account; she speaks of "feminine weaknesses," of care of the body, of troublesome tears, of the imagination, of penances, and of the whole process of growth and feminine development in the relational process with Christ.

Teresa's relationship with the nuns appears explicitly in the fifth dwelling places. The examples of love of neighbor are clear references to community relations (see the section titled "Love Has Taken Her out of Herself," in chapter 6 of this text). Love leads to treating her sisters as another "I," as if she herself were the needy one. Teresa models the self-surrender and love of a mother, and of a sister, loving her sisters and brothers as herself.

---

16. Women's relationships can be further explored in Teresa's other works as well, especially in *The Way of Perfection*, *The Book of the Foundations*, and the *Letters*.

Teresa's experience of God as Trinity, rooted in relationship, made her relationships in community possible, building up a communion of equality and mutuality, and connected to all creation.[17] In the sixth and seventh dwelling places, where Teresa describes these experiences, she is in a mode of full apostolic fruitfulness. From her experiences of Trinitarian love and mutuality, she lives and promotes a style of religious life based on communion and relationship, where feminine characteristics prevail above those of organization and hierarchies (see the section titled "Feminine Icons" in chapter 6 of this text).

Relationships between Men and Women

From the anthropological-theological perspective that Teresa outlines in *The Interior Castle*, a different understanding of the relationships between woman and man emerges, very different from the understanding and customs of her day. We recall that in the culture of sixteenth-century Spain, woman was regarded primarily as a servant to man, without value or significance in herself. Teresa understands the reality of women's submission in marriage, in society, and in the church. Like the butterfly of the sixth dwelling places, a woman must be liberated from the cultural and church "chains" that prevent her from announcing the reign of God in order to "save many souls." She asked that the Lord "make the great sea and the large river Jordan roll back and allow the children of Israel to pass" (IC 6.6.4).

The process that Teresa presents in *The Interior Castle* invites all those who read it to be men and women for others

---

17. "Let us say . . . that the Divinity is like a very clear diamond . . . of such a kind that it contains all things within itself; there is nothing that escapes its magnitude" (L 40.10).

in total self-giving, with no distinction between male and female, even though the way of giving may be different. She understood her being for the Other, or for others, not only in service to the male but also in service to all of humanity, with Christ as our model: in contrast to the men of his time, He made himself a slave, to serve and not to be served (this theme was dealt with in the section titled "Toward Mutuality: Love That Creates Solidarity" in chapter 6 of this text).

We have already commented on the themes of Teresa's prophetic dimension. Her contributions to woman-to-woman relationships bring us to the establishment of new relations between women and men in society and in the church. Certainly, the sociocultural reality in which Teresa lived is far from that of the twenty-first century. Yet unfortunately, in spite of the centuries that separate us, the social and ecclesial marginalization of women is still with us in many ways.

Because they are the feminine image of God, women show and re-present symbolically part of God's hidden mystery through what is increasingly necessary: their participation and communion in relationships that are mutual and equal at the ecclesial level. This will help bring about what the church represents symbolically in history, the new order of grace restored by Christ, in whom there is no distinction between women and men as children of God.

Female and Male Icons of Christ and of the Church

Teresa of Jesus presents a continuous reminder of the feminine and mystical dimension of the church as the bride of Christ. All of us, men and women, are called by baptism to live a relationship of total and fruitful surrender to Christ, the Way, the Truth, and the Life (Jn 14:6). The fundamental motivation of our apostolic service is, however, more than simply playing out an institutional role; it is love and friendship with Christ.[18] In this loving relationship, women are called to overcome those selfish tendencies that are part of connection and empathy; and men, to overcome their selfish tendencies of disconnection and isolation,[19] until both become women and men for the Other and for others, like the bride in love who surrenders herself completely, holding back nothing.[20]

The following graphic represents how each gender grows in relational maturity. While each gender's process of maturation is similar, from the point of view of purifying connectedness in relationships, they move in opposite directions, yet towards the same goal.

It is in the loving relationship with Christ where the whole person is transformed in him; only his love and friendship make it possible for women and men to become true icons of Christ, giving their lives as did he for the service of the church. We women and men form the Mystical Body of

---

18. In the homily for the beginning of his pontificate, Pope Emeritus Benedict XVI said, "There is nothing more beautiful than to know Him and to speak to others of our friendship with Him." Benedict XVI, homily, April 24, 2005, *L'Osservatore Romano*, Vatican City.

19. See Nancy Chodorow, "Gender, Relation and Difference in Psychoanalytic Perspective," in *Feminism and Psychoanalytic Theory*, 99–113 (New Haven, Conn.: Yale University Press, 1989); and Simon Baron-Cohen, *The Essential Difference: Men and Women and the Extreme Male Brain* (London: Penguin, 2003).

20. Religious conversion, according to Lonergan, "is total and permanent self-surrender without conditions, qualifications, reservations." Bernard Lonergan, *Method in Theology* (Toronto: University of Toronto Press, 1971), 240.

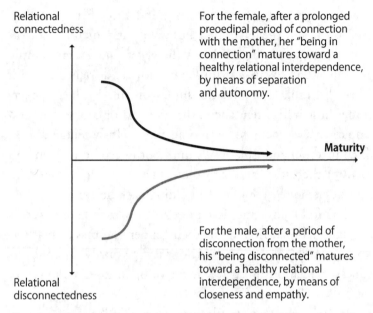

Process of maturation of the relational characteristics of gender

Christ,[21] but he alone is the head.[22] The image of God that is in all humanity refers to its original, that is, to God in the universal Christ. The feminine and masculine are redeemed in Christ, revealing his living face and representing it as icons shining in the world today.

Relationship with God and with Christ

As a woman, Teresa's way of knowing God is understandably feminine. Her knowledge of God begins with the relational

---

21. "Now you are Christ's body" (1 Cor 12:27).

22. "We should grow in every way into him who is the head, Christ" (Eph 4:15).

experience, characterized by a perception that is empathetic, intuitive, and subjective, and based fundamentally on her experience of the truth of faith. Her knowledge of God surpassed the rational and was kept alive by the Holy Spirit in a continuous relationship of "friendship with God." In the Second Vatican Council's Dogmatic Constitution on Divine Revelation (*Dei Verbum*), we find this form of revelation and knowledge: "Thus God, who spoke in the past, continued to converse with the spouse of his beloved Son. And the Holy Spirit, through whom the living voice of the Gospel rings out in the Church—and through it in the world—leads believers to the full truth and makes the word of Christ dwell in them in all its richness (see Col 3:16)" (DV 8).[23]

Teresa's understanding of prayer as a "matter of friendship" in an existential relationship reveals to us not only the relational characteristics of herself as a woman but also the relational characteristics of a God who communicates God's own self to his creatures, and who in his humanity enters into a relationship with his sisters and brothers at a level of equality and mutuality. With her mystical experience Teresa reveals faith content to us, giving new meaning to the content of revelation.

In *The Interior Castle*, Teresa writes a Christology beginning from the mystical, that is, from her own relational experience with Christ. As Karl Rahner tells us, "As much from the perspective of the fundamental theology as from the human point of view, it is perfectly legitimate for

---

23. Austin Flannery, ed., *The Basic Sixteen Documents of Vatican II* (Northport, NY: Costello Publishing, 1996).

a Christology to begin from our personal relationship with Christ."[24]

Teresa's contribution as a woman is that of a *Christopathy*, because her knowledge comes from the experience in an empathic relationship, through which she has entered into Christ's own feelings. She knows Christ because she shares his life and his mysteries; she feels with him, loves with him, suffers with him, rejoices with him, and later elaborates her reflection of faith as did Paul of Tarsus. She introduces us to a God who reveals himself as human, close, one like us; he makes himself a slave in order to manifest his love; His *Christophanies* (appearances of Christ after the Ascension) are in accord with our humanity. Teresa's relationship with God continues transforming her until she becomes like him and can experience the Trinity. From that experience, she reveals to us a *God who offers a relationship* and who wants to live in communion with his creatures. Teresa's Christophany invites us to enter into reflection, considering human pathos and, above all, contemplating Christ alive and present today in the human suffering that is both concrete and global, Christ in solidarity with the human race, sharing with those who have no hope, reclaiming for every human being his or her own dignity and deeper call. Following the thread of compassion and empathy that we discover in Teresa, we discover a love surpassing all reason, love surrendered by a God who lives in the midst of his creatures.

---

24. Karl Rahner and Wilhelm Thüsing, *Cristología. Estudio Teológico y Exegético* (Madrid: Ediciones Cristiandad, 1975), 21.

Epilogue

On finishing this study, we can say that taking into account the psychological human characteristics of woman, with her limitations and potentials, as well as her divine characteristics, as reflection and image of God, a process of human maturation has been envisioned that reveals the identity of woman as an icon of Christ, lovingly surrendered to the service of humanity, and an icon of the Espousal Church, which is sanctified in its deep relationship with the Lord. This is the mystique in Teresa of Jesus.

The path of appropriation of her identity as a woman from a perspective of totality, is developed from the relational perspective, taking into account the conscious and unconscious sociocultural conditioning that the concept of gender can take in itself. Here appears the beginning of her prophecy: a liberation and unmasking of cultural preconceptions that prevented her from realizing God's dream in it. Her whole life represents a new paradigm of women in the Church that continues to cry out to this day. In the middle of the persecutions she discovered the presence of Jesus in the poor and the little ones. The experience of God's love was woven in profound unity with the love of our sisters and brothers, in solidarity with the whole human race.

I think it is possible to consider this path as a proposal of feminine spirituality that helps unravel the commitment of women in the Church and in society. I strongly hope that this book is a useful new instrument for women and men who feel called to be mystics and prophets in our world. Now, at the end of these pages I want to evoke the memory of Teresa of Jesus, who discovered her image of a woman stamped on the same God, and looking so well painted, put in him her house and her dwelling place:

> "His Majesty takes delight in you. Don't let any earthly thing be enough to separate you from your delight, and rejoice in the grandeur of God; in how He deserves to be loved and praised; that He helps you to play some small role in the blessing of His name; and that you can truthfully say: *My soul magnifies and praises the Lord.*" (S 7.3)

Bibliography

Principal Sources of Teresa of Jesus

Ahlgren, Gillian. *Teresa of Ávila and the Politics of Sanctity.* New York: Cornell University Press, 1996.

Álvarez, Tomás. "Biografía e Historia." In *Estudios Teresianos.* Vol. 1. Burgos, Spain: Monte Carmelo, 1995.

———. *Cartas Santa Teresa.* Burgos, Spain: Monte Carmelo, 1979.

———. *Cultura de mujer en el s. XVI. El caso de Santa Teresa.* Burgos, Spain: Monte Carmelo, 2006.

———, ed. *Diccionario de Santa Teresa.* Burgos, Spain: Monte Carmelo, 2002.

———, ed. *Obras completas de Santa Teresa.* Burgos, Spain: Monte Carmelo, 2002.

———. *Santa Teresa a contraluz.* Burgos, Spain: Monte Carmelo, 2004.

———. "Santa Teresa y las mujeres en la Iglesia: Glosa al texto teresiano de Camino 3." *Monte Carmelo* 89 (1981): 121–32.

———. *Teresa de Jesús.* Burgos, Spain: Monte Carmelo, 2001.

Álvarez, Tomás, and Antonio Más. *Reproducción en facsímil del Castillo Interior.* Burgos, Spain: Monte Carmelo, 1990.

Álvarez Vazquez, José. *Trabajos, dineros y negocios. Teresa de Jesús y la economía del siglo XVI.* Madrid: Trotta, 2000.

Bañez, Domingo. "Censura en el autógrafo de la Vida de Sta. Teresa." In *Obras completas de Santa Teresa,* edited by Efrén de la Madre de Dios and Otger Steggink. Madrid: Editorial Católica, 1977.

Barrena, Jesús. *Teresa de Jesús, Una Mujer Educadora.* Ávila, Spain: Institución Gran Duque de Alba de la Diputación Provincial, 2000.

Bengoechea, Ismael. *Teresa y las Gentes.* Cádiz, Spain: Padres Carmelitas Descalzos, 1982.

Carrera, Elena. *Teresa of Ávila's Autobiography: Authority, Power and the Self in Mid-Sixteenth-Century Spain.* London: Legenda, 2005.

Castellano, Jesús. "La Belleza del Volto di Cristo nell'esperienza mística di Santa Teresa." *Rivista di Vita Spirituale* 54 (2000) 155–73.

Cerezo Galán, Pedro. "La Experiencia de la Subjetividad en Teresa de Jesús." In *La Recepción de los Místicos,* edited by Salvador Ros García, 171–204. Salamanca, Spain: Universidad Pontífica, 1997.

De Goedt, Michel. *Il Cristo di Teresa.* Vatican City: Libreriaeditrice vaticana, 1997.

De León, Luis. "Carta Dedicatoria a la Madre Priora Ana de Jesús y Religiosas Carmelitas Descalzas del Monasterio de Madrid." In *Los Libros de la Madre Teresa de Jesús Fundadora de los Monasterios de Monjas y Frailes Carmelitas Descalzos de la Primera Regla.* Madrid: la Imprenta Real, 1597.

————. *De la vida, muerte, virtudes y milagros de la Santa Madre Teresa de Jesús.* Salamanca, Spain: Universidad de Salamanca, 1991.

De León, Luis, and Félix García. *La Casada Perfecta.* Mexico City, Mexico: Aguilar, 1976.

Deneuville, Dominique. *Sainte Thérèse D'Ávila et le femme.* Paris: Editions du Chalet, 1963. Spanish translation, *Santa Teresa de Jesús y la Mujer.* Barcelona: Herder, 1966.

De Ossó, Enrique. La mujer grande: vida meditata de santa Teresa de Jesús, enseñando *come madre, maestra y doctora universal, con ejemplos y doctrina. Barcelona: Tipografia Católica, 1882.*

De Pablo Maroto, Daniel. *Dinámica de la Oración.* Madrid: Editorial de Espiritualidad, 1973.

————. "Santa Teresa y el Protestantismo Español." In *Perfil Histórico de Santa Teresa,* edited by Teófanes Egido, 147–48. Madrid: Editorial de Espiritualidad, 1981.

Dobhan, Ulrich. "Teresa de Jesús y la emancipación de la mujer." In *Actas del Congreso Internacional Teresiano,* edited by Teófanes Egido, 121–36. Vol. 1. Salamanca, Spain: Universidad de Salamanca, 1983.

Egido, Teófanes, ed. *Actas del Congreso Internacional Teresiano.* Salamanca, Spain: University of Salamanca, 1983.

————, ed. *Perfil histórico de Santa Teresa.* Madrid: Editorial de Espiritualidad, 1981.

————. "Santa Teresa y su condición de mujer." *Surge* 40 (1982): 155–275.

Frohlich, Mary. *The Intersubjectivity of the Mystic.* Atlanta: Scholars Press, 1993.

Garcia, Ciro. *Santa Teresa de Jesús: Nuevas claves de Lectura.* Burgos, Spain: Monte Carmelo, 1998.

García, Felix. *Obras completas castellanas de Fray Luis de León.* Madrid: Biblioteca de Autores Cristianos, 1991.

García-Albea, Esteban. *Teresa de Jesús, una ilustre epiléptica.* Madrid: Huerga y Fierro Editores, 1995.

Garcia Oro, José. "Reformas y observancias: crisis y renovación de la vida religiosa española durante el Renacimiento." In *Perfil Histórico de Santa Teresa,* edited by Teófanes Egido, 32–55. Madrid: Editorial de Espiritualidad, 1981.

Gili, Gustavo, ed. *Vida de la Madre Teresa de Jesús, Fundadora de las Descalzas y Descalzos Carmelitas por el Padre Francisco de Ribera.* Barcelona: Gustavo Gili, 1908.

González Casas, Maria Rosaura. *Teresa de Jesús, Memoria subversiva.* Barcelona: Ediciones STJ, 2005.

Herráiz, Maximiliano, ed. *Obras completas de Santa Teresa de Jesús.* Salamanca, Spain: Ediciones Sigueme, 1997.

Howells, Edward. *John of the Cross and Teresa of Ávila, Spain: Mystical Knowing and Self-hood.* New York: Crossroad, 2002.

Kavanaugh, Kieran, ed. *The Collected Letters of St. Teresa of Ávila,* 2 vols. Washington, D.C.: ICS Publications, 2001, 2007.

Kavanaugh, Kieran and Rodriguez, Otilio, eds. *The Collected Works of St. Teresa of Ávila,* 3 vols. Washington, D.C.: ICS Publications, 1976–1985, 1987, 2012, 2017

Llamas, Enrique. "Santa Teresa de Jesús ante la Inquisición Española." *Ephemerides Carmeliticae* 13 (1962): 518–65.

————— and others, eds., *Santa Teresa de Jesús Obras Completas*. Madrid: Editorial de Espiritualidad, 1976.

—————. *Santa Teresa de Jesús y la Inquisición Española*. Madrid: Consejo Superior de Investigaciones Cientificas, Instituto "Francisco Suarez," 1972.

—————. "Teresa de Jesús y la religiosidad popular." In *Perfil Histórico de Santa Teresa*, edited by Teófanes Egido, 57–94. Madrid: Editorial de Espiritualidad, 1981.

—————. "Teresa de Jesús y los alumbrados. Hacia una revisión del 'alumbradismo' español del siglo XVI." In *Actas del Congreso Internacional Teresiano*, edited by Teófanes Egido, 137–67. Vol. 1. Salamanca, Spain: Universidad de Salamanca, 1983.

Lopetegui, León. "Censura de la Orden de la Vida de Teresa de Jesús, por Francisco de Ribera, SJ." *Manresa* 16 (1944): 261–74.

Lopez Baralt, Luce. "Teresa de Jesús y el Islam. El símil de los siete castillos concéntricos del alma." In Mujeres de luz: la mística femenina y lo femenino en la mística, edited by Pablo Beneito, Lorenzo Piera, and Juan José Barcenilla, 53–75. Madrid: Trotta, 2001.

Marcos, Juan Antonio. *Mística y Subversiva. Teresa de Jesús*. Madrid: Editorial de Espiritualidad, 2001.

Más Arrondo, Antonio. *Acercar el cielo*. Cantabria, Spain: Sal Terrae, 2004.

—————. *Teresa de Jesús en el Matrimonio Espiritual*. Ávila, Spain: Institución Gran Duque de Alba de la Excma. Diputación Provincial, 1993.

Matus, Jill L. "Saint Teresa, Hysteria, and Middlemarch." *Journal of the History of Sexuality* 1, no. 2 (1990): 215–40.

McLean, Julienne. *Towards Mystical Union.* London: St. Paul's, 2003.

Navarro Puerto, Mercedes. *Psicología y Mística. Las Moradas de Santa Teresa.* Madrid: Ed. San Pio X, 1992.

Rahner, Karl. "La experiencia personal de Dios más apremiante que nunca." In *Teresa de Jesús Doctora de la Iglesia, Revista de Espiritualidad* 29 (1970): 310–13.

Ribera, Francisco. *La Vida de la Madre Teresa de Jesús: Fundadora de las descalzas y descalzos carmelitas.* Madrid: Edibesa, 2005.

Rossi, Rosa. *Teresa d'Ávila. Biografía di una scrittrice.* Rome: Editori Riuniti, 1983. Spanish translation, *Teresa de Ávila. Biografía de una escritora.* Barcelona: Icaria, 1984.

Royo Marín, Antonio. *Doctoras de la Iglesia: Santa Teresa de Jesús, Santa Catalina de Siena y Santa Teresa de Lisieux.* Madrid: Biblioteca de Autores Cristianos, 2002.

Ruiz Soler, Luis. *La personalidad económico-administrativa de la Santa Madre Teresa de Jesús.* Zarautz, Spain: Ed. Icharopena, 1970.

Silverio de Santa Teresa, ed. *Biblioteca Mística Carmelitana.* Vols. 1–3, 17. Burgos, Spain: Monte Carmelo, 1933, 1935.

Sérouet, Pierre, and Jerónimo Gracián. *Glanes: Quelques brèves additions de la main du Pére Gratien á la première biographie de Thérèse d'Ávila par le Père Francisco de Ribera.* Laval, France: Carmel de Laval, 1988.

Slade, Carole. *St. Teresa of Ávila: Author of a Heroic Life.* Berkeley: University of California Press, 1995.

Stein, Edith. *Il castello dell'anima: riflessioni sul Castello interiore di s. Teresa d'Ávila*. Florence, Italy: OCD, 1981.

Vázquez, Antonio. "Psicología y Teología en el Castillo Interior." *Revista de Espiritualidad* 165 (1982): 460–530.

Velasco, Juan Martín. "Búscame en tí—Búscate en mí. La correlación entre el descubrimiento del hombre y descubrimiento de Dios en Santa Teresa." In *Actas del Congreso Internacional Teresiano*, edited by Teófanes Egido, 800–834. Vol. 2. Salamanca, Spain: Universidad de Salamanca, 1983.

Vergote, Antoine. "Una mirada psicológica sobre la mística de Teresa de Ávila." In *Actas del Congreso Internacional Teresiano*, edited by Teófanes Egido Martinez, 883–96. Vol. 2. Salamanca, Spain: Salamanca University, 1982.

Walsh, Terrance G. "Writing Anxiety in Teresa's Interior Castle." *Theological Studies* 56 (1995): 251–75.

Watt, Ninfa. "El estilo de Santa Teresa en un mundo antifeminista." *Monte Carmelo* 92 (1984): 287–318.

Weber, Alison. "Spiritual Administration: Gender and Discernment in the Carmelite Reform." *Sixteenth Century Journal* 31, no. 1 (2000): 123–46.

———. *Teresa of Ávila and the Rhetoric of Femininity*. Princeton, N.J.: Princeton University Press, 1990.

Welch, John. *Spiritual Pilgrims: Carl Jung and Teresa of Ávila*. New York: Paulist Press, 1982.

Other Sources

Aquinas, Saint Thomas, Shapcote, Laurence and Sullivan, Daniel. *Saint Thomas Aquinas: the Summa Theologica Vols 1-2*. Chicago: Encyclopedia Britannica, 1990.

Arnold, Magda B. *Emotion and Personality*. New York: Columbia University Press, 1960.

Arnold, Wilhelm, Hans Jürgen, and Richard Meili, eds. *Lexikon der Psychologie*. Freiburg, Germany: Herder, 1980. Italian translation, *Dizionario di Psicologia*. Rome: Pauline Editions, 1990.

Aubenas, Roger, and Robert Ricard. "El Renacimiento." In *Historia de la Iglesia*, edited by Augustin Fliche and Victor Martin. Vol. 17. Valencia, Spain: EDICEP, 1974.

Baron-Cohen, Simon. *The Essential Difference: Men, Women and the Extreme Male Brain*. London: Penguin, 2003. Italian translation, *Questione di Cervello. La Differenza Essenziale tra Uomini e Donne*. Milan: Mondadoni, 2004.

Beauvoir, Simone de. *Le Deuxieme Sexe*. Paris: Gallimard, 1949. Italian translation, *Il Secondo Sesso*. Milan: Il Saggiatore, 2002.

Benedict XVI. Homily, April 24, 2005. L'Osservatore Romano, Vatican City.

Benjamin, Jessica. *Like Subjects, Love Objects: Essays on Recognition and Sexual Difference*. New Haven, Conn.: Yale University Press, 1995. Italian translation by C.M. Xella, *Soggetti d'amore: genere, identificazione, sviluppo erotico*. Milan: Cortina, 1996.

———. "The Question of Sexual Difference."*Feminism and Psychology* 12 (February 2002): 39–43.

————. *Shadow of the Other: Intersubjectivity and Gender in Psychoanalysis*. New York: Routledge, 1998.

Berdahl, Jennifer, and Cameron Anderson. "Men, Women, and Leadership Centralization in Groups over Time." *Group Dynamics: Theory, Research and Practice* 9, no. 1 (2005): 45–57.

Chodorow, Nancy. "Gender, Relation and Difference in Psychoanalytic Perspective." In *Feminism and Psychoanalytic Theory*, 99–113. New Haven, Conn.: Yale University Press, 1989.

Cordoba, Martin de. *Tratado que se intitula Jardín de las nobles doncellas*. Edited by Fernando Rubio. Madrid: Atlas, 1946.

De Moreau, Emma, Pierre Jourdá, and Pierre Janelle. "La Crisis religiosa del siglo XVI." In *Historia de la Iglesia*, edited by Augustin Fliche and Victor Martin. Vol. 18. Valencia, Spain: EDICEP, 1978.

Diana, Massimo. *Ciclo di vita ed esperienza religiosa*. Bologna, Italy: Edizioni Dehoniana Bologna, 2004.

Gilligan, Carol. *In a Different Voice: Psychological Theory and Women's Development*. Cambridge, MA: Harvard University Press, 1982.

————. "Remapping the Moral Domain: New Images of the Self in Relationships." In *Essential Papers on the Psychology of Women*, edited by Claudia Zanardi, 480–95. New York: New York University Press, 1990.

González Casas, Maria Rosaura. *La Casa se llenó del perfume*. Mexico City, Mexico: Ediciones Dabar, 2007.

————. *Mujer, tienda de encuentro, espacio de relaciones*. Barcelona: STJ Ediciones, 2004.

————. "Sexualidad y Desarrollo Integral. Perspectiva Femenina." *Diakonía* 26, no. 103 (2002): 24–50.

————. "Vida Consagrada: discípula, mística y profética. Crisis y nuevas perspectivas." *Revista Diakonia*, no. 122 (June 2007): 38–62.

Gran Enciclopedia Universal. Madrid: Espasa Calpe, 2004.

Ignatius of Loyola. *Ejercicios Espirituales. Autógrafo Español.* Madrid: Apostolado de la Prensa, 1979. English edition, *The Spiritual Exercises of St. Ignatius of Loyola.* Translated by Elder Mullan. New York: P. J. Kennedy & Sons, 1914.

Imoda, Franco. *Sviluppo Umano, Psicología e Mistero.* Casale Monferrato, Italy: Piemme, 1993.

Javierre, José M. *Juan de la Cruz, un Caso Límite.* Salamanca, Spain: Sigueme, 1991.

————. *La Jesuita Mary Ward.* Madrid: Libros Libres, 2002.

————. *Teresa de Jesús: aventura humana y sagrada de una mujer.* Salamanca, Spain: Sígueme, 2001.

John XXIII. *Pacem in Terris. Sulla Pace fra tutte le genti.* Vatican City: Edizione Paoline, 1963.

Kernberg, Otto. *Aggression in Personality Disorders and Perversions.* New Haven, Conn.: Yale University Press, 1992.

————. *Object Relations Theory and Clinical Psychoanalysis.* New York: Aronson, 1976. Italian translation, *Teoría della Relazione Oggettuale e Clinica Psicoanalitica.* Turin, Italy: Bollati Boringhiere, 1980.

Kiely, Bartholomew. *Psychology and Moral Theology.* Rome: Gregorian University Press, 1987.

Klein, Melanie. "Early Stages of Oedipus Conflict." In *The Writings*. Vol. 1, *Love, Guilt and Reparation and Other Works*, 186–98. London: Hogarth, 1975.

Lebeau, Paul. *Etty Hillesum. Un itinérair espirituel*. Namur, Belgium: Fidélite, 2000. Spanish translation, *Etty Hillesum. Un Itinerario espiritual*. Cantabria, Spain: Sal Terrae, 2000.

Lonergan, Bernard. *Method in Theology*. Toronto: University of Toronto Press, 1971.

Maccise, Camilo. *Un nuevo rostro de la Vida Consagrada*. Gasteiz-Vitoria, Spain: Instituto Teólogico de Vida Religiosa, 2004.

Meissner, William. *Ignatius of Loyola: The Psychology of a Saint*. New Haven, Conn.: Yale University Press, 1992.

Melquíades, Andrés. "Erasmismo y Tradición." In *Perfil histórico de Santa Teresa*, edited by Teófanes Egido, 95–117. Madrid: Editorial de Espirituálidad, 1981.

Mitchell, Juliet. *Psychoanalysis and Feminism*. New York: Basic Books, 2000.

O'Dwyer, Cáit. *Imagining One's Future: A Projective Approach to Christian Maturity*. Rome: Editrice Pontificia Università Gregoriana, 2000.

Pascal, Blaise. *Pascal's Pensées*. New York: E. P. Dutton, 1958.

Rahner, Karl. *Theologian of the Graced Search for Meaning*. Edited by Geffrey B. Kelly. Minneapolis: FortressPress, 1992.

Rahner, Karl, and Wilhelm Thüsing. *Cristología. Estudio Teológico y Exegético*. Madrid: Ediciones Cristianidad, 1975.

Ratzinger, Joseph. *Das neue Volk Gottes*. Düsseldorf, Germany: Patmos, 1969. Spanish translation, *El nuevo pueblo de Dios*. Barcelona: Editorial Herder, 1972.

———. *Die Letzte Sitzungs periode des Konzils*. Cologne, Germany: Bachem, 1966. Spanish translation, *La Iglesia en el mundo de hoy*. Buenos Aires: Ediciones Paulinas, 1968.

———. *La Fraternidad cristiana*. Madrid: Taurus, 1962.

Rizzuto, Ana Maria. "Approccio tecnico alle tematiche religiose in psicoanalisi." In *Psicoanalisi e religione. Nuove prospettive clinico-ermeneutiche*, edited by Mario Aletti and Fabio De Nardo, 184–215. Turin, Italy: Centro scientifico, 2002.

———. *The Birth of the Living God*. Chicago: University of Chicago Press, 1979.

———. "Processi psicodinamici nella vita religiosa espirituale." *Tredimensioni* 3 (2006): 10–30.

Ruano, Lucinio, ed. *San Juan de la Cruz. Obras completas*. Madrid: Biblioteca de Autores cristianos, 1974.

Rulla, Luigi M. *Anthropology of the Christian Vocation*. Rome: Gregorian University Press, 1986.

"Sancta Teresia a Iesu Doctor Ecclesiae." *Ephemerides Carmeliticae* 21 (1970): 1–3.

Schökel, Luis Alonso. *Símbolos matrimoniales en la Biblia*. Pamplona, Spain: Verbo Divino, 1999.

Sicroff, Albert. *Les controverses des status de "puretè de sang" en Espagne*. Paris: Didier, 1960. Spanish translation, *Los estatutos de limpieza de sangre. Controversias entre los siglos XV–XVII*. Madrid: Taurus, 1985.

Six, Jean Francois. *Vie de Charles de Foucauld.* Paris: Editions du Seuil, 1962.

Urist, Jeffrey. "The Rorschach Test and Assessment of Object Relations." *Journal of Personality Assessment* 41, no. 1 (1977): 3–9.

———. "Validity of the Rorschach Mutuality of Autonomy Scale: A Replication Using Excerpted Responses." *Journal of Personality Assessment* 46, no. 5 (1982): 450–54.

Velasco, Juan Martín. *El fenómeno místico. Estudio comparado.* Madrid: Editorial Trotta, 1999.

Winnicott, Donald. "Transitional Objects and Transitional Phenomena." *International Journal of Psychoanalysis* 34, no. 2 (1953): 89–97.

Index

About Us

ICS Publications, based in Washington, D.C., is the publishing house of the Institute of Carmelite Studies (ICS) and a ministry of the Discalced Carmelite Friars of the Washington Province (U.S.A.). The Institute of Carmelite Studies promotes research and publication in the field of Carmelite spirituality, especially about Carmelite saints and related topics. Its members are friars of the Washington Province.

The Discalced Carmelites are a worldwide Roman Catholic religious order comprised of friars, nuns, and laity—men and women who are heirs to the teaching and way of life of Teresa of Avila and John of the Cross, dedicated to contemplation and to ministry in the church and the world.

Information about their way of life is available through local diocesan vocation offices, or from the Discalced Carmelite Friars vocation directors at the following addresses:

Washington Province:
1525 Carmel Road, Hubertus, WI 53033

California-Arizona Province:
P.O. Box 3420, San Jose, CA 95156

Oklahoma Province:
5151 Marylake Drive, Little Rock, AR 72206

Visit our websites at:

www.icspublications.org   and   *http://ocdfriarsvocation.org*